Eight Stone Gates

Taking Thoughts Captive

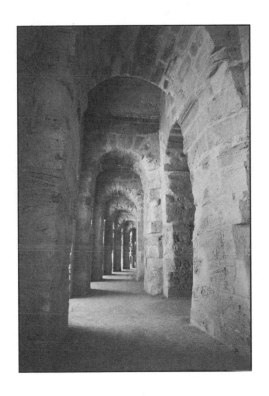

DAN MANNINGHAM

Eight Stone Gates
Taking Thoughts Captive
by Dan Manningham

Scripture references are quoted from
The New International Version of the Bible
and where noted,
The King James Version,
The New King James Version,
The New American Standard Bible,
and the English Standard Version.

Cover design by Melanie Schmidt
Cover photograph by Gay Ayers
(www.gayayers.com)
Used by permission

ISBN 1-885904-75-4

PRINTED IN THE UNITED STATES OF AMERICA
BY
FOCUS PUBLISHING
Bemidji, Minnesota

Eight Stone Gates

Taking Thoughts Captive

DAN MANNINGHAM

Dedication

To Fran:
51 years
7 children
28 grandchildren
9 states
4 countries
19 homes
Countless blessings

To: "Corn Muffins and Apple Butter"
And
"Extra Croutons"
(you know who you are)
Thanks for the wisdom

Table of Contents

Introduction

"Every man has a train of thought on which
he travels when he is alone. The dignity and
nobility of his life, as well as his happiness,
depend upon the direction in which that
train is going, the baggage it carries, and the
scenery through which it travels."
-Joseph Fort Newton

Brothers, stop thinking like children.
In regard to evil be infants,
but in your thinking be adults.
1 Corinthians 14:20

Scripture has much to say about thinking: what God thinks
about; what we think about God; and what we think about
ourselves and others. It talks about thoughts that separate us
from God, thoughts that draw us closer to God, thoughts that
initiate a slide into rebellion and sin, and thoughts that are
simply inappropriate for those who claim to have a personal
and intimate relationship with the God of eternity.

It is appropriate that Scripture talks about our thoughts
because they move through our mind like a river flowing between
its banks. They never end. They rush along in a flood of mental
concepts and desires and images that never stops. We are always
thinking. It is our very nature. We anticipate, remember, plan,
consider, evaluate, reflect, imagine and suppose. We think.

The issue is what do we think about? One of Jesus' most
frequently asked questions was, "What do you think?" Good
question.

In the midst of this we are assured that we have the ability
to control our thoughts and we are commanded to do just that.

Paul told the Corinthians, *"We take captive every thought to make it obedient to Christ" (1 Corinthians 10:5).* No one said it would be easy, but Scripture says we are to be the master of our thoughts and not the victims.

Further, there is one clear and pertinent command in Paul's letter to the Philippians, which specifies eight topics or themes that should define our thinking. *"Finally, brothers, whatever is true, whatever is noble, whatever is right, whatever is pure, whatever is lovely, whatever is admirable—if anything is excellent or praiseworthy—think about such things" (Philippians 4:8).*

It is easy to gloss over these simple imperative statements, but they stand as clear injunctions, unmistakable directives, regarding our thought life, which we ignore at our peril.

But there is abundant reason to regulate our thinking beyond the simple fact that Paul says so. Sound thinking is essential for sound living. Disciplined thoughts are the prerequisite for an ordered and satisfying life. What we think inevitably becomes what we do. It is a biblical principle that is a demonstrable life principle. Your thoughts determine your actions. Consider Proverbs 23:7; Matthew 15:16-19; Luke 6:43-45, and Proverbs 4:23.

Fortunately, taking our thoughts captive is not a painful task. We can control our thoughts, and those eight topics from Philippians 4:8 are each pleasant in their own way. When our thinking is channeled into those themes we reap the benefits of clarity and vision and enjoyment that are not possible with undisciplined and disobedient thoughts.

This is not intended to be manipulative mind control. In reality, this is a mental and spiritual discipline designed for health, strength, and the relief of anxieties that tend to creep into our lives. It is the simple process of harmonizing our thoughts with our convictions. It is one important dimension of living a life consistent with our belief.

Whatever is true, noble, right, pure, lovely, admirable, excellent or praiseworthy, think on these things.

When I was a child, I talked like a child,
I thought like a child, I reasoned like a child.
When I became a man,
I put childish ways behind me.
1 Corinthians 13:11

Eight Stone Gates

Chapter One

Building Walls

"Before I built a wall I'd ask to know
What I was walling in or walling out."
-Robert Frost

**You see the trouble we are in: Jerusalem lies in
ruins, and its gates have been burned with fire.
Come, let us rebuild the wall of Jerusalem, and
we will no longer be in disgrace.
Nehemiah 2:17**

In the sixth century before Christ, the nation of Judah had declined into a corrupt and impoverished country with little spiritual or political strength. They had neglected the temple worship of Yahweh in favor of pagan gods. Those practices involved violence, twisted sex and human sacrifice, including the sacrifice of infants thrown into a furnace. The rituals were morally repulsive and deeply offensive to God who had so lovingly cared for this people through at least 1500 years. From the height of grandeur and respect 400 years previously, Judah and Jerusalem had degenerated into a moral, economic and military failure.

In 609 BC, the last honorable king, Josiah, was killed in battle by an Egyptian arrow on the plains of Megiddo. Ironically, this same real estate will host the final and ultimate battle of Armageddon where the last evil king will be defeated. The last worthy king and the final wicked leader each dying on the same piece of land. Interesting …

Josiah was succeeded by three of his sons. The first, Jehoahaz, reigned only three months before he was dethroned by King Neco of Egypt and carried away to that country in disgrace.

Jehoahaz was succeeded by Jehoiakim, who is described as "doing evil in the eyes of the Lord" and was dethroned by Nebuchadnezzar and taken to Babylon in shackles. The final two kings were both described as wicked, weak men and the nation finally fell to the Babylonians under King Nebuchadnezzar in 586 BC, who deported most of them to Babylon where they lived out their lives in bondage to him.

For the next 141 years, the proud nation of Judah and its once impressive capitol of Jerusalem were left to the jackals and snakes and thorn bushes along with a few, weary and thoroughly dispirited people who had been left behind because they were too weak or old. The once proud city of David and Solomon had come to a pitiful end. Think of Berlin or Tokyo in 1945 and you will have an idea.

When Jerusalem fell in the sixth century, the thick stone walls and secure gates were destroyed and with them all hope of protection from thieves and bandits, wild animals and foreign armies. Among the piles of rubble and memories, the Jews who remained were defenseless and subject to the whim of any roving group of thugs or hungry animals.

Without defense and commerce, Jerusalem was a place of confusion and anarchy controlled and maintained by the corrupt and thuggish Babylonian occupiers. It was a place of chaos, dominated by hooligans and vulnerable to any perverse influence.

But help was on the way.

During those dark years, thousands of Jews lived in captivity, first to the Babylonians and then to the Persians when that empire conquered Babylon. Some of those Jews had risen to prominence in the royal court in Persia and served as important officials there. One of them was Nehemiah, who served as cupbearer to the Persian King Artaxexes I. Understand that cupbearer to the king was a highly respected position of trust and put Nehemiah in close, personal contact with the king on a daily basis.

In late 445 BC, one of Nehemiah's brothers returned to the capital city of Susa from a visit to Jerusalem and told Nehemiah about the wretched conditions in that once beautiful city. Nehemiah was so moved for his Jewish people and his homeland that he risked his life to ask King Artaxexes for permission to return to Jerusalem and rebuild the walls. To Nehemiah's great delight, the king granted his request and even provided a military escort for his protection.

When he arrived in Jerusalem, Nehemiah inspected the walls and announced, *"You see the trouble we are in: Jerusalem lies in ruins, and its gates have been burned with fire. Come, let us rebuild the wall of Jerusalem, and we will no longer be in disgrace"* (Nehemiah 2:17).

During the next 52 days, Nehemiah rallied the people of Jerusalem to repair the walls and 12 individual gates. It was an astonishing accomplishment in so short a time and a serious defeat for the enemies of the Jews and their holy city who taunted and threatened them every day. Each one of those gates had to be framed in stone and then hung with massive, hand-crafted wooden doors that could be firmly barred against unwanted intruders. When the work was completed, Jerusalem was as secure as it could be. It was surrounded by stone walls in which stone gateways were framed and hung with stout wooden doors. In that way, only desirable people and products could enter the city. In most ancient, walled cities it worked like this ...

When the gates were open, guards would be stationed at each one to monitor the traffic, especially the people and animals traveling into the city. Anyone who approached a gate was subject to search and questioning by the guards. A farmer who came with figs to sell in the market would be allowed entry because his purpose was right and just. A drunk who wanted to find more wine would be turned away because he was certain to cause trouble. And any hostile force would be barred from entry by closing and barring the gate.

The gates were the city's filter to allow what was good and prevent what was not in the same way that the water filter on your tap allows clean water to flow out but traps harmful particles and contaminants before they can enter your glass. Further, in Jerusalem the gates each had specific functions. There was a horse gate, a sheep gate, a water gate, a fish gate, etc. Each gate was designated for a primary purpose, although if they were left unprotected, anything could enter through any gate.

> "Good thoughts are blessed guests,
> and should be heartily welcomed,
> well fed and much sought after.
> Like rose leaves they give out a sweet
> smell if laid up in the jar of memory."
> -Charles Spurgeon

> **Finally, brothers, whatever is true, whatever**
> **is noble, whatever is right, whatever is pure,**
> **whatever is lovely, whatever is admirable—**
> **if anything is excellent or praiseworthy—**
> **think about such things.**
> **Philippians 4:8**

In the book of Philippians, the apostle Paul prescribes eight filters or gateways to order our thinking. He was aware that we all struggle with anxieties that create bad thoughts, wrong thoughts, inappropriate thoughts and, sometimes, evil thoughts. He knew that we also struggle with anxious and fearful thoughts and so he gave us a list of eight standards with which to regulate our thinking.

If you think of your mind as a walled city you can think of these eight themes described by Paul as eight stone gateways through which your thoughts can be policed. You can imagine these gateways as being—in their own way—like the gates built for Jerusalem where guards were stationed to monitor the traffic and forcibly prohibit anything that was detrimental. These eight stone gateways are meant to be the filters that prevent impurities and poisons, thugs and enemies from entering your mind while allowing good and constructive thoughts to flow freely.

It is all a nice idea, but it does not work without our active participation. We must install the gates and we must provide the muscle to police the gateways just as Nehemiah did when Jerusalem was open and vulnerable. It is a life-long mission to exclude the harmful and welcome the beneficial. Paul's instruction in Philippians 4:8 is easy to read and even memorize (highly recommended), but his words are of little value without some diligent work with stone and mortar, wood and bronze, or, in this case, with mental discipline and moral courage.

This book attempts to describe those eight mental themes as eight stone gateways to our mind that can regulate the traffic like the gates to Jerusalem. You will have to lay up the stones of personal dedication and hang the gates of daily self discipline, but the end result is pleasing to God and beneficial to you.

Think of your mind as being surrounded by a wall of God's protection. He has provided that wall as a means for all who count Jesus Christ alone as their Savior and Lord to exclude sinful thoughts while leaving gateways for right thoughts to enter. Remember that the city is always under attack by powerful and destructive forces that constantly seek entrance, but the goal is to keep a strong and diligent guard and filter our thoughts through these eight stone gates. You will learn that:

- The Truth Gate is where we allow only information that is carefully validated and certified to be true. The Truth Gate is for admitting thoughts of what is.
- The Noble Gate is where thoughts of courage, generosity and honor are admitted. The Noble Gate is for admitting the good that could be.
- The Right Gate is for thoughts that are proper and appropriate for a son of the King. The Right Gate is designed for thoughts of what should be.
- The Pure Gate is designed for thoughts that are free of impurities and contaminants. The Pure Gate is for thoughts of what ought to be.
- The Lovely Gate is for inspiring thoughts of beauty and delight, both physical and moral. The Lovely Gate is for thoughts of God and His creation.
- The Admirable Gate is for thoughts of things that are inspiring and deserving of high praise and approval. The Admirable Gate is for thoughts of those things of which we are capable.
- The Excellent Gate is for thoughts of things that possess outstanding qualities; things that are remarkably good. The Excellent Gate is for thoughts of those things to which we should aspire.
- The Praiseworthy Gate is for thoughts of things that are highly commendable; things that are worthy of applause and tribute. The Praiseworthy Gate is for thoughts of things that are inspiring and motivating.

Nehemiah rebuilt the walls and gates of Jerusalem in 52 days. During part of that time the Jews were under such immediate threat that they worked with a tool in one hand and a weapon in the other.

If your mind has become a spiritual wasteland because the walls have been battered down by armies of evil thoughts, it is not too late. Just like Nehemiah in Jerusalem, you too can rebuild the walls and gates in 52 days, or less. You may need to fight with one hand and build with the other, but there is no other way to restore the walls and gates so that you can begin to guard against thoughts that are angry, lustful, bitter, obscene, spiteful, corrupt, wrong, impure, critical, dark and sinful.

None of this will be easy but you do have powerful promises to lean on:

- I can do everything through him who gives me strength (Philippians 4:13).
- The LORD is the stronghold of my life—of whom shall I be afraid? (Psalm 27:1b).
- Sovereign LORD, my strong deliverer, who shields my head in the day of battle—do not grant the wicked their desires, O LORD; do not let their plans succeed (Psalm 140:7).

There are countless other promises of God's help and strength throughout the Bible. You will discover, that and the ones you find for yourself will be the most meaningful and enduring. Search them out. Start in the book of Psalms, but don't stop there.

"Temptation usually comes in through a door
that has deliberately been left open."
-Arnold Glasow

I went past the field of the sluggard ...
the ground was covered with weeds,
and the stone wall was in ruins.
Proverbs 24:30-31

This is not a book about behavior. It is not about how to be a better wife, husband, employee, citizen or financial steward and yet it is about all of those things and more. This is a book about broken walls and burned gates of the mind and the plan God has set forth to rebuild them. It is a book about repairing the mind and restricting what goes into it with the belief that what goes in will inevitably come out.

Perhaps your thinking has been captive for some time and when you survey your mind you realize that the walls have been breached and there is considerable damage. Just like city walls and gates, there are two things that destroy the gates and walls of your mind: war and neglect. Psychological warfare over issues of besetting sin can simply destroy the walls by brute force. It is spiritual warfare in the power of the Holy Spirit that can bring victory. Neglect will allow the walls and gates to fall into disrepair with the same corrosive result over time.   If your walls and gates have been breached or ruined, they can be repaired. Jerusalem was worse and Jerusalem was restored to great beauty and honor. Your mind can be also, whether that involves the eviction of one scoundrel or an entire army, whether that involves simple repairs or complete reconstruction.

It is time to start.

"Thoughts lead on to purposes; purposes
go forth in action; actions form habits;
habits decide character; and
character fixes our destiny."
-Tryon Edwards

**We demolish arguments and every pretension
that sets itself up against the knowledge of
God, and we take captive every thought
to make it obedient to Christ.
2 Corinthians 10:5**

Chapter Two

The Problem with Thinking

Thinking is easy.
Right thinking is hard work.
-Anonymous

**A simple man believes anything,
but a prudent man gives thought to his steps.
Proverbs 14:15**

In 1904, the French sculptor, August Rodin, presented his bronze sculpture titled, "The Thinker" (Le Penseur), to the public. It is a large statue of a man seated on a rock and bent forward with his chin resting on the back of his right hand and his left forearm on his left knee. It is certainly the best known of all Rodin's many, brilliant works and most people are exposed to it in some fashion during their early school days.

"The Thinker" is an icon of contemplation or meditation. It is a symbol of learned minds pondering the mysteries of the universe, or of a simpler mind trying to balance his checkbook. It is a brilliant statue both in its artistic style and in its concept of something that we can all understand: thinking.

We are prone to describe certain people as "thinkers" if we believe they have a tendency to analyze and probe difficult issues, but the truth is that we are all thinkers. We think all the time; it never stops. We think about the guy in the next cubicle, the neighbor's new landscaping, the bills that are due, our children's future, our parent's approval, our career potential, our favorite sports team, politics, war, the past, the future and the unknown. We have thoughts of lust, greed, envy, bitterness, revenge, criticism and we occasionally have thoughts of sacrificial love, forgiveness, patience and tolerance.

It is not a matter of whether we think, but what we think about. We think.

This is an interesting concept because there is no direct opposite to thinking; there is no real antonym to the word "think." There is no "unthink" or "dethink." For the human being thinking just is. We think, we assume, we reflect, we meditate, we consider, we ponder, we imagine.

So the real question is, "Do we think in ways that are pleasing to God and therefore beneficial to us? Do we entertain thoughts that are selfish, mean spirited, or otherwise sinful? Or, do we just aimlessly, randomly think?"

Thinking is easy. Right thinking is hard work.

> "Thoughts may be bandits. Thoughts
> may be raiders. Thoughts may be invaders.
> Thoughts may be disturbers
> of the international peace."
> -Woodrow Wilson

For as he thinks in his heart, so is he.
Proverbs 23:7 (NKJV)

When Solomon wrote that proverb he chose an unusual Hebrew word for "think," which is used only one time in the Old Testament. It does mean to "think," but it carries an unusual connotation since the Hebrew word "sha'ar" comes from a root which means to open as a gate keeper would open his gate. Accordingly, you could translate this short proverb as, *"For as a man opens the gates of his mind and allows thoughts into his heart, so is he"* (paraphrase of Proverbs 23:7).

Think of Eve in the Garden of Eden. She was a thinker. She knew that God had carefully instructed them to eat anything they wanted with only one exception. He said they could have it all, every delicious, juicy, savory item in His creation except the fruit of that one tree way over there in the middle of the great garden where they really didn't have any need to go anyway. She knew that. She thought about that and for some time she did not allow other thoughts to enter her mind. Her wall of protection was intact and her gates were guarded. *"For as a man opens the gates of his mind and allows thoughts into his heart, so is he."*

Then one day she was confronted with a new and tantalizing thought, introduced by a charming and eloquent stranger. He argued that God didn't know what He was talking about—she wouldn't really be harmed by this succulent fruit—and she would actually benefit from it.

Suddenly there was a new thought at the gates. At that moment she could allow the enemy to enter her mind or slam the gates shut to unwanted and harmful thoughts. Her choice of thinking at that moment would determine her choice of behavior. She could entertain the errant thought, that mental virus, and eat the forbidden fruit, or close the gate to a lie and decline to eat the fruit, remaining obedient to the One who had given them everything.

Eve did a poor job of guarding the gates, as did her husband. She allowed an evil cancer named sin to enter the gate and infect her mind. The infection weakened her defenses and she ate the fruit with catastrophic consequences for herself, her children and all her children's children forever. It all started with the enemy at the gate and a defense that failed. *"For as a man opens the gates of his mind and allows thoughts into his heart, so is he."*

> "You are today where your thoughts
> have brought you; you will be tomorrow
> where your thoughts take you."
> -James Lane Allen

Eight Stone Gates

**Enter through the narrow gate. For wide is
the gate and broad is the road that leads to
destruction, and many enter through it. But
small is the gate and narrow the road that leads
to life, and only a few find it.
Matthew 7:13-14**

We humans are thinking creatures, but our record in that department is not good. Some tend to extremes and see all things as either black or white. Others are never able to discriminate and so they entertain any and all thoughts, even when there is evil involved.

Some spend considerable energy on mental criticism of whatever they dislike or idolatrous fascination of something they love too much. Some simply deny the reality of difficult situations in order to avoid painful decisions and relations. Some exaggerate every problem into a supposed crisis. Some accept cruel and deceptive labels for themselves and others: fat, ugly, dumb, ignorant, stupid or worthless.

In countless ways we open our mind gates to thoughts that are false, lowly, wrong, corrupt, ugly, inferior, shameful or unworthy. That is the enemy's list of eight preferred and recommended thoughts. They are the opposite of God's approved list of topics (Philippians 4:8) and they are widespread.

<u>False</u>: Jacob lied to his father, Isaac, about who he was when Isaac asked for his favorite food on his deathbed. What Jacob told his father was not *true*.

<u>Lowly</u>: The priest and the Levite walked right past the injured Samaritan. Their thoughts were miserly and self-centered, not *noble*.

<u>Wrong</u>: The Pharisees thought they could please God with good behavior. Their entire theology was not *right*.

<u>Corrupt</u>: David gave up his integrity for a night with Bathsheba. His thinking at that time was not *pure*.

18

Ugly: The serpent that tempted Eve was condemned to slither on his belly in the dust although he had up to that time been *lovely.*

Inferior: Ananias and Sapphira promised the monetary value of a piece of property to the church but when they saw how much money was involved they kept back some for themselves. Their gift was deceitful and therefore not *excellent.*

Shameful: Peter denied Christ three times. His thinking was craven and spineless. It was not an *admirable* moment for him.

Unworthy: Jonah skulked off toward Spain when he had been given a mission to Nineveh by God. His thoughts and actions were certainly not *praiseworthy.*

But be cautious not to be too critical of these characters from the pages of God's Word since they are each a small snapshot of what we all have done at one time or another. Without strong walls and well-guarded gates false, lowly, wrong, corrupt, ugly, inferior, shameful and unworthy thoughts creep into our mind and set up housekeeping.

Accordingly, it is no mistake that Paul transmitted God's approved thinking in those eight clear and opposite categories of true, noble, right, pure, lovely, excellent, admirable and praiseworthy. This is the very same God who knows the thoughts and intents of our heart, who lived in the flesh as a human being subject to all of our temptations and who delights to give us simple guidelines for holy living: ten commandments for Godly behavior, 15 dimensions of genuine love (1 Corinthians 13:4-7), six elements of personal conduct (Colossians 3:12-14), etc.

"Men have the power of thinking
that they may avoid sin."
-Saint John Chrysostom

Eight Stone Gates

Where is the wise man? Where is the scholar?
Where is the philosopher of this age?
Has not God made foolish the
wisdom of the world?
1 Corinthians 1:20

It is a sweet thing to know how God wants us to think. It is helpful to understand the explicit areas of thought that God would like us to entertain. It is clear that He is not impressed with intelligence or education or clever thinking. He is interested in much simpler things which do not preclude the others. God is not in any way opposed to brilliance or creative thinking or extensive education but He would like all of those thoughts to be filtered through gates that admit only what is true, noble, right, pure, lovely, excellent, admirable and praiseworthy.

You can study nuclear physics or microbiology or quantum mechanics and stay within those simple guidelines. You could also study systematic theology, poetry and philosophy and miss them altogether.

Be sure you don't see this as a legal checklist to certify your acceptability to God since that can only be accomplished through the perfect sacrifice of His son, Jesus. We are saved by grace. There is no behavior checklist for admission to heaven, but God has made known many things that are pleasing to Him and for that reason alone we should be interested and committed to thinking as He has described. And when we think *"on those things"* we naturally produce the fruit that is pleasing to Him.

"When I work, I work hard,
When I sit, I sit still,
When I think, I fall asleep."
-Anonymous

**Have nothing to do with godless
myths and old wives' tales;
rather, train yourself to be godly. For
physical training is of some value, but
godliness has value for all things.
1 Timothy 4:7-8**

Right thinking is difficult and noble work, certainly not something to be left to the professionals. It is the mental equivalent of a physical workout and, accordingly, can be tough work, but enormously rewarding.

When Paul instructed Timothy to "train" himself he used the Greek word "gumnazo" which is the basis for our English word "gymnasium." Paul and Timothy were well familiar with the concept since the Grecian culture that permeated their world included a strong emphasis on physical training. You can see that in much of Paul's writing where he talks about racing and boxing and competing. Accordingly, I think it would be fair to loosely translate Paul's instructions to Timothy like this, *"Look, Tim, you already know something about physical exercise, but now I want you to exercise your mind in Godly thinking. Your body is the temple of the Holy Spirit and worthy of sound maintenance, but your thinking is where the hard work must be done. Pump some mental iron. Work at it until you sweat. No mental pain, no spiritual gain."*

Godly training for the believer in Jesus Christ must naturally involve some meditation on the truths of Scripture, the greatness of God and the immensity of our salvation. But understand that meditation is not some mysterious activity associated with obscure religions. Meditation is simply the process of examining a thing thoroughly.

When you worry about a problem you are meditating on all of the possible outcomes and difficulties that could arise from that problem. When you anticipate your next vacation you are meditating on all of the expected pleasures and enjoyments. We all meditate. It is a more focused and intense form of thinking, but we all do it. We meditate about supper, our work, taxes, football and shopping. We think and meditate as an integral part of our being and, accordingly, we want to exercise that thinking (meditation) in Godliness.

Think about Scripture. It is a rich source of material for meditation. This volume of 66 books is not some accidental collection of ancient writings. It is the "breathed out" word of God, specially crafted to reveal God's glory and His purpose for mankind. Its central theme is God's plan of redemption for a race of people who are rebellious by nature. Within that theme, it is the story of normal people, confronted with moral and physical dilemmas and finding God's divine favor.

In this volume are innumerable tales of cowardice, deception, adultery, idolatry, war, surrender, murder, child abuse, drunkenness and more. There are also great accounts of courage, honesty, faithfulness, moral integrity and loyalty. And woven through from Genesis 3:15 to the very end of Revelation is the scarlet thread of hope and redemption for a lost and sinful people who deserve judgment and punishment. Behind it all is the cross on which the Lamb of God paid the penalty for my sins. Where else in all of literature do you find grace, forgiveness and unconditional love tightly woven through all the normal failures of human living and thinking? It is worth some serious mental exercise.

Think about the greatness of God. He has no beginning and no end. He is accountable to no one. He is supreme over everything. There is no limit to His power, His knowledge, His place or His time. He is God. Further, He cares about you and He proved it. Think about that. Meditate on it.

"To be blind is bad, but worse it is
to have eyes and not see."
-Helen Keller

The LORD gives sight to the blind,
the LORD lifts up those who are bowed down.
Psalm 146:8

Think about the immensity of salvation. We, who are separated from God by our sinful nature, have been offered a reprieve. God sent His Son as a sacrifice for our sin in the same way the Jews slaughtered sheep and goats and sprinkled their blood on the altar in the temple to atone for their sins. The difference is that Jesus was the Lamb who paid the penalty for all the sins of the entire world and all we have to do is receive that. *"Behold the Lamb of God who takes away the sin of the world"* *(John 1:29).*

It is a worthy topic for meditation even though it defies all of our logic and human wisdom. It is nicely expressed in the story of a blind man in John's gospel. I love this guy.

He had been blind from birth, a pathetic invalid with no hope in a poor country with no welfare system. A man condemned to ridicule and poverty. Blind. Helpless.

When the disciples asked Jesus about the cause of this blindness, He said it was there to display the work of God since He, Jesus, was the light of the world. The man was blind as an example of darkness to contrast with Jesus' light. Then Jesus made some mud with His saliva and put it on the blind man's eyes. When he had washed it off, the blind man could see!

And then the carping began. The local folk and the self-righteous Pharisees just couldn't believe that Jesus had cured the blindness. First, some of his neighbors denied that this guy was the former blind man. It must be mistaken identity.

Then the Pharisees disputed the idea that Jesus could cure anything. The healer must be a charlatan.

Then some others questioned his parents about his former blindness. Probably never was blind.

Picture this guy who has been blind from birth, suddenly beholding all of the color and richness of God's world, astounded by the beauty of light and shade and harassed by skeptics who want to ridicule this obvious miracle.

Imagine this guy listening to the cynical questions about an event that is intensely real to him who was blind from the moment of his birth until his breakfast that day and now seeing with 20/20 vision at lunch. He is frustrated because they are trying to deny what is so obvious to him and in his frustration he says this, *"I don't know (about all that stuff). One thing I do know. I once was blind but now I see"* (John 9:25).

Now think of it in a more personal way. Jesus is the Light of the World. He came to open spiritual eyes. He came to reveal light and truth. He came to bring salvation.

You want to ask me how that can be. How a sinner can be turned from darkness to light?

You ask me if I was really born spiritually blind.

You ask me penetrating philosophical questions about life and eternity? Go ahead, and here is my answer.

"I don't know (about all that stuff). One thing I do know. I was blind but now I see."

It is a beautiful thing to meditate upon. Once I was blind to God's goodness and wisdom and authority and now I see. Once I was blind to my personal, moral corruption and now I see. Once I was blind to God's plan for reconciliation and now I see. Think about it.

"Thinking is the hardest work there is,
which is probably the reason
why so few engage in it."
-Henry Ford

**Brothers, stop thinking like children.
In regard to evil be infants, but in
your thinking be adults.
1 Corinthians 14:20**

One of Jesus' most frequent questions to His followers was, "What do you think?" Clearly He recognized that there was a process going on inside those heads and that they had some control over it.

What do we think? We think about a collective list of personal desires, personal grievances and personal memories. We think constantly because thinking is easy, but right thinking is hard work. Right thinking is a familiar theme in Scripture:

- "Think like (spiritual) adults" (1 Corinthians 14:20).
- "Think soberly" (Romans 12:3).
- "Think righteously" (Psalm 119:7).
- "Think prudently" (Proverbs 13:16).

Peter concluded his second letter with these words, *"This is now my second letter to you. I have written both of them as reminders to stimulate you to wholesome thinking" (2 Peter 3:1).* His point is that he had written two entire letters with the single motive being to stimulate them to right thinking.

When Paul wrote his short letter to the church in Philippi he recognized that their thoughts were important because they influenced their actions. He also made a direct connection between their anxieties and their thought processes and he gave them a list of eight themes around which to organize their thoughts: whatever is true, noble, right, pure, lovely, admirable, excellent and praiseworthy. And then he concluded with a command to *think on these things*. And although Paul didn't say it, thinking is easy, but right thinking is hard work.

"Life does not consist mainly—or even
largely—of facts and happenings. It consists
mainly of the storm of thoughts that is forever
blowing through one's head."
-Mark Twain

When I was a child, I talked like a child;
I thought like a child, I reasoned like a child.
When I became a man, I put
childish ways behind me.
1 Corinthians 13:11

Chapter Three

The Gate of True Thoughts

"The truth, the whole truth
and nothing but the truth."
-Legal phrase from at least 1300AD

Buy the truth and do not sell it.
Proverbs 23:23

The truth gateway demands considerable vigilance since we live in a fallen world that is saturated with lies and rumors and half truths; innuendo, insinuation and vain imagination all trying to gain entrance. When Paul says *think about what is true*, the meaning from the original Greek is, well, whatever is actually true. What is. What is verifiable, demonstrable or provable; what is not legend and story, rumor and gossip, hearsay and anecdote. That which conforms to the reality of things.

It is an interesting word, actually. The root of the Greek word used here for "truth" is a word that means to "lie hidden," to "purposely conceal" as we do when we are deceptive. That word is then equipped with a prefix which means "not" so that the final word that Paul used for "truth" in this verse literally means "not concealed" and, thus, true. It is an inverse but creative way of making the point that truthfulness of character means refusing to conceal the truth in its details. I like that.

It is an unfortunate fact that much of the world's mischief is caused by well-meaning people who act in good faith by thoughts and convictions that are entirely wrong. That oath that is administered to all who give testimony in a court of law involves three elements that apply well to Paul's command in Philippians 4:8:

- The truth: what the witness experienced or saw.
- The whole truth: not leaving any material out.
- Nothing but the truth: definitely no lies.

This is not a deep philosophical concept. We are to think about "the truth, the whole truth and nothing but the truth." We are to think about things that are true and exclude the rest.

Amazingly, we love things that are rumors and gossip and we spread them everywhere. The workplace and the neighborhood and the internet are filled with things that are not true. They are not all harmful lies, but we certainly live in a world that is saturated with unfounded rumors, like:

- An egg can be cooked by placing it between two activated cell phones.
- Chewing gum takes seven years to pass through the human digestive system.
- A tooth left in a glass of Coca Cola will dissolve overnight.
- Elvis is alive and working at a Seven Eleven in Butte, MT.

None of those are true, but we love that stuff and it gets worse. We also love gossip about friends and relatives and the rich and famous. We fixate on stories about bug-eyed extraterrestrials and three-headed babies and the Bermuda Triangle. And we dabble with religious ideas that have no basis other than tradition and hearsay.

Recently the world has been fascinated by the "DaVinci Code," which speculates about a love affair between Jesus and Mary Magdalene that produced a child. Like gossip, people were drawn to it and bought over 8 million copies. Many accept it as being thoroughly believable when it is nothing but the product of a vivid and seriously anti-Christian mind. The DaVinci Code has no more foundation for truth than an Elvis sighting. It is fiction, like Sponge Bob or James Bond or Barbie and Ken.

We entertain thoughts and ideas that have no basis in reality and those thoughts are the cause of considerable difficulty. Note that fiction and fantasy in art and conversation are fine as long as they are understood to be fiction and expressed as such. It is not that we must live without any sense of invention or imagination; it is that we must be careful to distinguish between what is true and what is imaginary. When we *think about what is true*, the goal is to separate fact from fiction; not to always exclude fiction, but to be very careful that fiction does not successfully masquerade as truth.

God knew that we would be fascinated with rumor and gossip and because of that he motivated Paul to include this clear verse about our thinking and to begin the list with *whatever is true*. Determine what is actually true and think on these things. True thoughts. Thoughts that can be confirmed. Authentic, legitimate, genuine, correct thoughts. *Think about what is true.*

> "Truth is truth 'till the end of reckoning."
> -Shakespeare

> **For I am convinced that neither death nor life,**
> **neither angels nor demons, neither the present**
> **nor the future, nor any powers, neither height**
> **nor depth, nor anything else in all creation, will**
> **be able to separate us from the love of God that**
> **is in Christ Jesus our Lord.**
> **Romans 8:38-39**

There is such a large spectrum of false, bogus, counterfeit ideas that it would not be possible to mention all of them in this chapter. There are, however, some examples that might be helpful. Remember that the goal here is to exclude thoughts from our mind that are not true and admit only those that are valid, authentic and accurate. And yes, it is fine and sometimes good to imagine, visualize and dream about creative and fanciful ideas, but those must be isolated and excluded from the mental storage lockers of truth.

One false thought that lingers outside the mental gate of every believer in Jesus Christ is the thought that questions our security as a child of God. This thought tries to gain entry so that it can disrupt your relationship with God by persuading you that God doesn't exist; that He doesn't care; that He has discarded you; that there never was a relationship between you and God in the first place. This thought is named "doubt" and it is vicious and cunning and persistent.

I read a story about a farmer who was a Christian man. He had come to know Jesus Christ as his Savior and Lord many years earlier and had gone on to live a life of faith that God is, that His Son died to take the penalty for his sin, that his hope of eternal life with God was based on the simple truth that he was truly a sinner saved by grace.

Nevertheless, this poor man was plagued by doubts. They gathered at the truth gate frequently and demanded entrance. These doubts would arrive when he was plowing or harvesting or doing routine chores. His thoughts would be interrupted by doubts about God and his relationship with Him. These doubts were all lies, but they were forceful and persistent.

One day while driving his tractor he was particularly troubled by these doubt-lies and so he drove to the barn with a new idea. He found an old stake and fastened a small board to it. He wrote the date on that board and pounded the stake into the ground on the south side of the barn in the bright sunshine. He then took the time to make a firm mental note that on that day he believed. On that day at that moment he knew that he was a child of God and that his eternity was secure because of Christ's work on the cross and no other. In that moment his doubts were overcome with truth.

After that day, when doubts came, he could say with confidence to the enemy, "Go look on the south side of the barn and see that little sign board with a date on it. See that? On that day I knew my relationship with God was and would be permanent. On that day I knew, and although you may bother me with doubt at this moment, I can always see that sign board and remember that *'nothing can separate me from the love of God.'*"

Perhaps you need to set a tangible signpost of truth to your own security as a child of God. I liked this farmer's story so much that I followed his example. Today there is a small boulder on the east bank of Chickenboro Brook in the White Mountains of New Hampshire where many years ago I chiseled "9 Aug 79" and a cross. When the enemy attempts to storm my gate of truth, I send him to that rock which bears the truth of my salvation and will forever. On that day I knew that my Redeemer lived and that he would never leave me nor forsake me. You can threaten my truth gate today but I know the truth and it is more permanent than that New England granite.

"To treat your facts with imagination is one
thing; to imagine your facts is another."
-John Burroughs

**Send forth your light and your truth,
let them guide me.
Psalm 43:3**

One set of lies that frequently attacks the truth gate is the fertile imagination of "what if—." Parents will recognize this in the form of a teenage child who is 15 minutes late for curfew. In those moments multiple lies seek entrance to the mind.

- Surely he has had a terrible accident and is lying bloody and unconscious in the mangled car.
- Maybe he has been using drugs and is stoned and lying in a gutter somewhere.

- Perhaps she has been mugged or robbed or worse.
- Certainly she has encountered grave danger and is helpless, or even now being rolled into surgery to repair some traumatic injury.

In those moments it seldom occurs to us that the car malfunctioned, that traffic was backed up or that she was delayed by an act of mercy for someone else.

We are assaulted by thoughts of tragedy, crisis and disaster when we really have no information whatsoever. In those moments it is difficult to filter our thoughts, but it is important to focus on what is true and not on what might be.

There is a Chinese proverb about an old man who lived with his only son. This man owned very little other than his horse, which was his source of income and transportation and physical security. The man was fond of his horse and often let him graze freely in the meadow which lay on the border of a neighboring country.

One day a servant reported to the old man, "The horse is missing! It must have wandered across the border into the neighboring state." His friends felt sorry for him. They said that this must be bad luck, but the old man said, "Do not say this is bad luck. Say only that the horse is gone."

A few months later, a strange thing happened. Not only did the missing horse return home safely, it brought back with it a truly fine and valuable mare from across the border.

When his friends heard the news, they congratulated the old man on his good luck. But the old man said, "Do not say this is good luck. Say only that my horse is back and another with him."

One day, when the old man's son was riding that beautiful mare, he accidentally fell off, broke his leg, and was crippled so that he would never walk normally again. Many friends came to comfort the old man, but the old man was not disturbed by the accident. "Do not say this is misfortune. Say only that my son has fallen and cannot walk."

A year later, when the neighboring state sent troops across the border, all the young and strong men were drafted to fight the invaders, and many of them were killed. The old man's son was not drafted because he was crippled and so his life was spared. Many friends declared the old man's good fortune to be a blessing. "Do not say that my fortunes have been blessed. Say only that my son has been spared."

Say not that the bank will repo your home and that you will have to live under a bridge, say only that today you cannot pay the mortgage.

Say not that my diabetes/high blood pressure/heart murmur/asthma will ruin my life in a few years. Say only that today I am okay and that God is able to provide for me.

Naturally, we are not to be naïve and avoid responsibility and wise behavior, but true thinking will exclude those flights of painful imagination.

The truth gate is reserved for thoughts of what is, what is authentic and valid and reliable.

> "Christianity, if false, is of no importance, and
> if true, of infinite importance. The only thing it
> cannot be is moderately important."
> -C.S. Lewis

Eight Stone Gates

**You shall know the truth and the
truth shall set you free.
John 8:32**

There is no limit to the number of lies that linger outside the truth gate. Some will leak in because our defenses are not perfect, but the goal always is to *"think whatever is true."* But there is an even bigger problem with identifying truth.

Ironically, we live in an age in which all truth is denigrated. It is considered perfectly fine and even fashionable to believe that there is no real truth; that truth is simply what you want it to be. The current academic phrasing is that "truth is a construct." Truth is said to be constructed out of your experience and prior teaching and personal imagination; truth, they say, is private and individual.

During the past 40 years, there has been a vigorous debate in academic circles regarding the truth of science. One side of this debate insists that science is no more than a product of our personal experience and imagination. They contend that science is a cultural product rather than an objective analysis of an absolute reality.

Imagine believing that verifiable scientific truth is simply a set of cultural opinions! This thinking has become popular among academics who deny any God or any other truth. It is bizarre thinking, since one must assume that such thinkers would demand that their plumber believe in the truth of gravity if he is to unclog a drain and their mechanic must believe in the truth of Newtonian physics if he is expected to repair their car.

Constructed truth is a view that conflicts directly with the realities of life and with the Bible, which holds that truth is an absolute and cannot change.

In everything, God has made it plain that there is truth. There is physical and practical truth that pertains to our every day activities. There is scientific truth that helps us to understand the intricacies of God's creation. And there is spiritual truth that binds them all together.

There is the central truth that God is good and wise and sovereign—all three, at all times. There is the eternal truth that answers the three eternal questions of all philosophical examination:

- <u>Where did it all come from</u>? From God, the self-existent One, who created it.
- <u>What went wrong</u>? Man rebelled against God's simple standards and introduced moral blight (sin) into the world.
- <u>What is the solution</u>? Christ came to accept the penalty for all of that moral blight (sin) for all who would believe.

God has made it plain in a thousand ways that there is truth—practical truth, scientific truth and spiritual truth—and that one of the gates of our mind is meant to admit only thoughts of truth. *"Whatever things are true."*

But wait! It turns out that these eight gates are not arranged around the perimeter of the wall so that thoughts can be admitted through a single gate. In Philippians 4:8, the gates are arranged in a sequence so that any thought should pass through each of the gates, one gate at a time.

"Surely you desire truth in the inner parts" (Psalm 51:6). So now that you have considered your thoughts for their truthfulness you can't stop there. Even when they are truthful, they must also be noble, right, pure, lovely, excellent, admirable and praiseworthy.

Eight Stone Gates

"The question is not whether a doctrine is
beautiful but whether it is true. When we
wish to go to a place, we do not ask whether
the road leads through a pretty country, but
whether it is the right road."
A.W. and J.C. Hare

**Stand firm then, with the belt of truth
buckled around your waist.
Ephesians 6:14**

Chapter Four

The Gate of Noble Thoughts

"A noble man compares and
estimates himself by an idea which is
higher than himself; and a mean man,
by one lower than himself."
-Henry Ward Beecher

**But the noble man makes noble plans,
and by noble deeds he stands.
Isaiah 32:8**

We are instructed to first pass our thoughts through the gateway of truth. Now, this truth has the very broad meaning of truthfulness of character; but, of course, character is lived out in minute details, so the truth here includes all the particular niceties of veracity and authenticity and accuracy that were described in chapter one. But, then, the idea of truth circles back through those details to the wide concept of candor; overall honesty; sincerity of character.

Once our thoughts have been vetted through that gate they must pass further and even stricter standards. Truthfulness is only the beginning. It may be true that your cousin is morbidly overweight and poorly self-disciplined and known for his belching and scratching, but entertaining those thoughts may not be noble and right and pure because your cousin is also a living soul, destined for an eternity of one kind or another and needful of truth and love.

So now we approach the next gate called "noble." Whatever is noble. Think about noble things. Your Bible translation may use the word "honest" or "honorable." Some translations use the English word "grave" in the sense of serious and important.

The directive here is that your thoughts have a quality that is noble and momentous and worthy of reverence in God's eyes. It is not some flimsy code of "nobility" that emerges from human tradition but an honor that can stand the test of eternity. It is noble in the very best sense. Noble as Christ was noble in all that He did. Noble as in being majestic and awe inspiring in a way that invites and attracts.

As difficult a word as it is to define, it all comes down to something pretty simple. Whatever is noble. Think about noble things. It need not be any more complicated than that.

> "There is no more noble occupation in
> the world than to assist another human being
> —to help someone succeed"
> -Alan Loy McGinnis

> **Be devoted to one another in brotherly love.**
> **Honor one another above yourselves.**
> **Romans 12:10**

Truly noble thoughts and actions are rare because they always involve self-denial. It is not really possible to be noble without thinking about God and others first.

Joseph (Jacob's son) was noble in denying the advances of Potiphar's wife. It was a noble thought and a noble deed because Joseph denied his natural appetite for carnal pleasure in favor of protecting Mrs. Potiphar's reputation and Mr. Potiphar's honor. It was an honorable thought because it transcended human desire and focused on God's glory and the benefit of someone else, even at Joseph's expense.

Joseph (Mary's husband) was noble when he silently and obediently married Mary despite her pregnancy. It was a noble and honorable thing to obey God's instruction and marry a woman who was pregnant by some other means. Joseph was not thinking of himself at that moment, but of his God and his betrothed. Very honorable. Very noble.

I remember being the object of a noble deed. It was 1962 in Guantanamo Bay, Cuba.

In that year, I was a Navy pilot based aboard the USS Lake Champlain (CVS-39). We had been anchored in Guantanamo Bay for several days enjoying the tropical weather and the limited pleasures of that confined naval base. There was not much to do at Gitmo and what there was centered on beer and fishing. Guantanamo Bay was teeming with fish, including sharks, and one afternoon I watched some sailors haul a six-footer out of the water.

Their ship was anchored in the middle of a lovely bay and liberty boats carried eager sailors back and forth from the shore base. Liberty boats were 50-foot open boats with bench seats for about 200 people. They were operated by crews of three men with a "Boat Officer" in command.

Now, in order to understand the concept you should know something about Navy culture. The three crewmen were perfectly capable of operating the boat without supervision, but the Navy assumed that any such vessel must have an officer in charge because officers are always in charge whether they know anything or not. There was a "Boat Officer" assigned to each boat as the functional commander. He stood in the middle of the boat on a little elevated pulpit that allowed him a clear view of things and he, well …, he stood there. That was it. He was purely a figurehead, a flunky.

On the night in question I was the designated lackey. I was the assigned boat officer for the last shift which included the last liberty boat back to the ship for the night.

I was a young naval aviator at the time. I knew little about airplanes and nothing about boats. Nevertheless, I was given the rare opportunity to command a seagoing naval vessel over three miles of sheltered water, so I stood in my pulpit and tried to look confident and commanding although I doubt anyone was persuaded. Everyone knew that boat officers were chumps. They were symbols of authority without any means of exercising that authority. We were unprotected and unarmed. We were targets for any possible rebellion and we were without defense. That was me: Chief Chump in charge.

As men loaded onto the boat at the pier I was not surprised to see that this last boat of the night included a large percentage of inebriated sailors. When the boat began its short passage out to the ship I could sense a rebellious spirit among several men seated in the bow section. Soon I heard references to "the boat officer" and then some comments about "the boat officer" in the same sentence with the word "overboard." It was turning ugly. I could swim and I had a life vest but it was very dark and I remembered that shark.

About half-way down to the ship some of the guys in that group stood up and started toward me. One said it openly, "Let's throw the boat officer overboard." Suddenly he had a significant number of followers and there was a surge of mutinous, drunken sailors toward my station. I was toast; shark toast.

Just as my options narrowed down to nothing I heard a deep voice behind and below me say, "Don't you worry 'bout nothing, Mr. Manningham. We gonna take care of this." When I looked, it was a Petty Officer named "A.C." Clark, a sailor who sang brilliantly at the ship's occasional talent shows where I sometimes held the position of MC. We had met briefly on those few occasions.

A.C. was a black man and an exemplary sailor. He had intelligence and discipline and quiet dignity, not to mention a very large and muscular body. As I looked around, several of A.C.'s black friends were arranged around the pulpit with their arms crossed and their faces set. They were a truly formidable guard although vastly outnumbered. Despite the numbers the tide immediately turned. Suddenly the mutiny was over and the rest of the trip was uneventful. I would live another day.

Now think about that. They were five black sailors who determined to defend a white officer during a time when the Navy was still plagued with racism. There were very few black officers and those few were assigned to lesser duties. Further, to my knowledge, there were no black pilots and even the black sailors were not well received by most. There was no "official" racism, but it was certainly a time when blacks were not treated as equals. Nevertheless, A.C. and his friends made the noble decision to put themselves at considerable risk and stand up to a mob of 50 or more drunken sailors to defend a skinny, insignificant, white, junior officer who had no way of ever repaying the favor.

Thanks A.C. Thanks for the protection that night in Guantanamo Bay and thanks for your example of noble thinking and noble action. *"The noble man makes noble plans, and by noble deeds he stands" (Isaiah 32:8).* Whatever is noble. Think about noble things.

> "No person was ever honored for what
> he received. Honor has been the
> reward for what he gave."
> -Calvin Coolidge

**Do not repay anyone evil for evil. Be careful to
do what is right in the eyes of everybody.
Romans 12:17**

Noble thoughts are beautiful because they are so rare and so wholesome. It is not common to encounter such honorable thoughts and deeds on the interstate or the subway or in the workplace, but they do exist and they are like fine pieces of art when we have the opportunity to observe them.

Choosing to think about whatever is noble is like savoring an art piece, and it is helpful to have a gallery of noble thoughts and deeds as examples when we are challenged to produce one of our own. Maybe you would like to formulate that noble thought, but you aren't sure what it would look like. It might help if you had some beautiful pictures to study. My experience with Petty Officer Clark and his friends is a small one, but there are many more and some of those are large canvases.

One of those beautiful portraits of noble thinking is a painting of Jim and Elisabeth Elliot. These two young people were missionaries in the jungles of Ecuador in 1956 when Jim was murdered by members of the Waorani tribe even as he and four others were attempting to contact them peacefully. They were simply run through with spears and some were mutilated by the very people they were trying to help.

Elisabeth was then left a young widow and mother of one. Two years after the murders, Elisabeth moved with her three year old daughter to live in the village of Waorani, with the people who had murdered her husband. Think about that: ministering grace to your husband's murderers. She was motivated by the noble thought that the Waorani were a people in need of the Gospel of Christ and that their need was more important than her well being. She was also familiar with her husband's defining belief, *"He is no fool who gives what he cannot keep to gain that which he cannot lose."* It doesn't get much nobler than that. Whatever is noble. Think about noble things.

"Every noble crown is, and on earth will
forever be, a crown of thorns."
-Thomas Carlyle

**And being found in appearance as a man, he
humbled himself and became obedient to
death—even death on a cross!
Philippians 2:8**

But there is one noble thought that led to one noble deed that exceeds all others. That deed is the cruel death of God's Son on a Roman cross as the only possible means of pardoning sin.

This deed is so commonly mentioned that is easily loses its gravity. We wear cross jewelry and hang decorative crosses from our rear view mirrors and on our front doors and we see them atop countless churches. In western culture, the cross is such an ordinary sight that it subtly loses any meaning. And yet, that symbol memorializes the single most noble thought and deed ever to exist.

Think about noble things. Surely there is no example more noble, and more honorable than the sovereign God sending His Son to die for me. I was spiritually blind and He gave me sight. I was morally diseased and He brought healing. I was lame and He taught me to walk. I was hungry and thirsty and He gave me eternal food and drink. And all of this He did by grace, mercy, kindness and compassion.

Whatever is noble. Think about noble things. But there is more. We must also think about what is right.

"I long to accomplish a great and noble task,
but it is my chief duty to accomplish humble
tasks as though they were great and noble"
-Helen Keller

**But the seed on good soil stands for those with
a noble and good heart, who hear the word,
retain it, and by persevering produce a crop.
Luke 8:15**

Chapter Five

The Gate of Right Thoughts

"For right is right, since God is God
And right the day must win.
To doubt would be disloyalty,
To falter would be sin."
-F.W. Faber.

Open for me the gates of righteousness;
I will enter and give thanks to the LORD.
This is the gate of the LORD through
which the righteous may enter.
Psalm 118:19-20

Once we have inspected our thoughts for their truth and honor we should look them over to see if they are right. *Whatever is true, noble, right .... Think about these things.*

Unfortunately, that word "right" has multiple meanings in English so it would be good to have a working definition of the Greek word Paul uses as we strive to admit only "right" thoughts through this third gateway.

The Greek word used here means "right" in the sense of "just," or "fair." The basic meaning assumes a standard of behavior that is recognized. A related word is used for "righteousness." So, when Paul tells us to think about what is "right," he is telling us to think about things that are equitable and ethical by God's standards. There is a comparable Hebrew word that is used in the Old Testament. Right and fair and just and righteous are important attributes for the thoughts we want to admit into our minds. This gate is where we screen out thoughts that are biased or prejudiced or unfair.

Children have a highly developed sense of what they think is right or, as they would say, "fair." So does God. But, we children and God often have very different opinions of exactly what that is. And even our convictions about what is right and fair are easily influenced and easily compromised without the clear and disciplined influence of Godliness in our thinking.

"Rightness expresses in actions what
straightness does in lines; and there can no
more be two kinds of right action than there
can be two kinds of straight lines."
-Herbert Spencer

**There is a way that seems right to a man,
but in the end it leads to death.
Proverbs 14:12**

Stanley Milgram was a young psychologist at Yale University in the 1960s. During those years he conducted experiments on human obedience that relate directly to the biblical concept of "right" and "fair", the concept of an accepted standard by God or man. The core of the experiment was that an ordinary citizen (you or me) would be instructed to inflict pain on another person simply because he was ordered to by an authority figure. This was a scientific assessment of whether average people would obey authority, even when called on to do something that was clearly contrary to what they believed to be "right."

The experiments measured a human being's willingness to obey an authority figure when instructed to perform acts that conflicted with his personal conscience. Although Milgram never phrased it this way, it is reasonable to say that the experiment measured whether a person's concept of "right" or "fair" was sufficiently well formed to insure right and fair behavior under stress.

When Paul instructs us to *think about what is right* he is not urging us to simply reflect on those virtues but to process them through our mind gate so that they will influence our behavior after they have been admitted. Milgram's experiments shed considerable light on that concept. Have we thought about *what is right* sufficiently to produce behavior that is fair and just?

"The line between good and evil runs directly
through the heart of every man and woman."
-Aleksandr Solzhenitsyn

**Create in me a clean heart, O God;
And renew a right spirit within me.
Psalm 51:10**

The experiments were conducted in the following fashion: Subjects in the experiment were told that they would be participating in a scientific study of memory and learning. They were compensated by the hour.

The setting was two small rooms with a wall between them. The subject of the study, who Milgram referred to as the "teacher," sat at a console with 30 small levers, each one corresponding to an additional 15 volts of electricity. The "learner," who was really an actor, was in the small booth on the other side of the wall seated on a chair which the teacher was told would administer electrical shocks when the levers were moved. The teacher and learner could communicate but could not see each other. In some of the experiments the learner made a point of explaining that he had a heart condition. The teacher was supervised by another actor who wore a white lab coat and played the role of the scientific administrator of the experiment. He was the authority figure.

Eight Stone Gates

Bear in mind that the "teacher" was really the subject of this experiment and was being tested and observed to see how compliant he or she was when instructed to do something that conflicted with personal conscience, with convictions of what was right and fair. Both of the other participants, the "learner" and the "scientist" were actors who simply played out the roles they had been assigned as a means of creating the environment for the "teacher" to be evaluated. Incidentally, the teacher was given a sample of the electric shock that the learner would supposedly receive during the experiment so that he was fully aware of what he would be asked to do.

Once the learner had been introduced and seated on the hot seat the teacher was instructed to read a list of word pairs to him. After reading the list of word pairs the teacher was then instructed to read the first word of a pair and four possible answers. (Remember, he thinks this is a study of memory and learning). In the booth, the learner then pressed a button to respond to these multiple choices. If the answer was incorrect the teacher was instructed to shock the learner, beginning with the first level of electric shock. As the experiment proceeded, the teacher was instructed to administer the next higher level of voltage to each successive wrong answer. In response to this shock a hidden tape recorder played recorded human sounds which were meant to simulate appropriate human responses to the voltage level, beginning with moans and groans and progressing with the level of voltage to shrieks that would be associated with excruciating pain. The teacher, of course, was convinced that there was a shock because he had experienced a real one in that very same chair before the experiment began, but in truth there was none. It was all a sham to measure the teacher's willingness to hurt someone just because he was told to do so. *Think about what is right.*

Naturally, some of the "teachers" expressed their discomfort with administering progressively higher levels of pain, but they were told progressively:

- Please continue, or
- The experiment requires that you continue, or
- It is absolutely essential that you continue, or
- You have no other choice, you must go on.

If the subject (teacher) still wanted to stop after all four of these verbal instructions the experiment was halted. Otherwise, it was not stopped until the maximum "450 volt shock" had been administered 3 times.

As the voltage increased, the tape recorded responses became more intense and the learner/actor would bang on the wall and complain about his heart condition. At a certain level, all responses from the learner/actor would ominously cease.

Prior to the actual experiments, Milgram's faculty associates and graduate students unanimously agreed that very, very few of the subjects would be willing to inflict the maximum voltage. The actual predicted percentage was 1.2%. In Milgram's first set of experiments 65% of the participants did administer the maximum voltage even though many felt very uncomfortable doing so. Only one absolutely refused to continue before the 300 volt level. These results have been verified by several similar tests since that time.

Milgram summarized the experiment in his 1974 article, "The Perils of Obedience" and that summary included this passage, *"Stark authority was pitted against the subject's (teacher's) strongest moral imperatives (what he thought was right and fair) against hurting others, and, with the subject's ears ringing with the screams of the victims, authority won more often than not."* (Parentheses inserted by me.)

Eight Stone Gates

"Let us have faith that right makes might
and in that faith let us to the end dare
to do our duty as we understand it."
-Abraham Lincoln

**The righteous care about justice for the poor.
Proverbs 29:7**

It is no wonder that Paul instructed us to *Think about what is right. Think about such things.*

Stanley Milgram's experiments focused on human obedience even when instructed to cruelty. But things are worse than that. Because we do not naturally dwell on *"what is right"* but on what is convenient or comfortable or easy, there are countless stories of human cruelty which could have been prevented by *thinking about what is right.*

In Germany in the 1930s and 1940s, millions of good, "Christian" people chose the easy path of denial and collaboration rather than the difficult and risky path that would have been the result of right, just, fair thinking. During the Nuremburg trials that followed WWII, the constant plea by Nazi officials who systematically murdered Jews and Gypsies and handicapped people was that they were "just following orders." In fact, those trials are the very thing that inspired Stanley Milgram to conduct his ground breaking experiments in human obedience.

During the 19th Century and before, countless "good" people bought and sold human beings because it was convenient and profitable and because they had not carefully turned their minds to thinking about what was right.

During the 20th Century tens of millions of unborn babies have been ripped from their mother's womb and sacrificed to human convenience because mothers and politicians and even church leaders have not given serious thought to what is right and fair and just as opposed to what is convenient. *Think about what is right.*

One of the tragic stories of deficient right thinking occurred in March of 1964 in the Queens Burrough of New York City. At 3:15 a.m. on the morning of March 13th, Kitty Genovese arrived home and parked her car about 100 feet from the front door of her apartment. As she walked that short distance she was attacked by Winston Mosley and stabbed twice in the back. Mosley's attack on Kitty Genovese continued over a 30 minute period during which her screams and pleas for help were heard by several people. One man turned up his radio in order to drown out the screams. Others apparently closed their windows to dull the sounds. No one went to her aid. Some were rumored to have said, "I didn't want to get involved." One neighbor apparently yelled out the window to "Let that girl alone," but then ignored the rest of the attack. Kitty Genovese died without help because as many as 38 people who heard her pleas were deficient in right thinking.

Ten years later, 25-year old Sandra Zahler was beaten to death on Christmas morning in an apartment of the building which overlooked the site of the Genovese attack. Neighbors again said they heard screams and a fierce struggle but did nothing. *"For as he thinks in his heart, so is he"* (*Proverbs 23:7, NKJV*).

If we are to think about what is right and fair and just, it must be a habitual thinking that leads to a change of perspective, or, as some would say, a change of heart.

"It is the mission of the teacher, not to make
his pupils think, but to make them think right."
-H.L. Mencken

The LORD loves righteousness and justice.
Psalm 33:5

Eight Stone Gates

Policing our thoughts so that they are carefully vetted through the "Right Gate" is a wise and obedient activity. It is what Paul instructed us to do, and it is not only pleasing to God, but He has promised, beneficial to us. Right thoughts lead to righteous character and there are multiple promises regarding that:

- Blessings crown the head of the righteous (Proverbs 10:6).
- The memory of the righteous will be a blessing (Proverbs 10:7).
- The mouth of the righteous is a fountain of life (Proverbs 10:11).
- The mouth of the righteous brings forth wisdom (Proverbs 10:31).
- The wages of the righteous bring them life (Proverbs 10:16).
- The tongue of the righteous is choice silver (Proverbs 10:20).
- The lips of the righteous nourish many (Proverbs 10:21).
- The prospect of the righteous is joy (Proverbs 10:28).
- The way of the LORD is a refuge for the righteous (Proverbs 10:29).
- The righteous will never be uprooted (Proverbs 10:30).
- The lips of the righteous know what is fitting (Proverbs 10:32).

When we carefully guard our thoughts, permitting only those that fit through the gates of true and noble and right, we not only change our mind, but our heart. Excluding unjust and unfair thoughts clarifies our thinking when we are exposed to difficult circumstances.

Onboard United Airlines flight 93 on September 11, 2001, Todd Beamer, one of the innocent passengers, had clearly entertained a steady diet of "right thoughts" which led him to mobilize and lead a heroic effort to overpower the hijackers.

While others were restrained by the authority and threats of the hijackers, Todd was motivated by a higher level of thinking about what would be right, fair and just. His thinking prompted his heroic actions. His heroic actions prevented a far bigger tragedy. *Think about what is right.*

But, there is more. We must also think about what is pure.

"Associate reverently, as much as you can,
with your loftiest thoughts."
-Henry David Thoreau

The LORD loves righteousness and justice.
Psalm 33:5

Eight Stone Gates

Chapter Six

The Gate of Pure Thoughts

"A pure mind in a chaste body is
the mother of wisdom."
-Jeremy Taylor

Everyone who has this hope in him purifies
himself, just as He is pure.
1 John 3:3

So far we have passed our thoughts through the Truth Gate,
the Noble Gate and the Right Gate. It is now time to examine
those thoughts for their purity. This is the Pure Gate.

Purity is a highly regarded quality. We love pure water, pure
air, pure-blooded animals, pure wool clothing and pure gold.
Pure is good.

The Greek word Paul uses here means "clean" in a moral
sense. It can mean "modest," "innocent" or "chaste." It derives
from another Greek word often translated "holy."

Apparently the English word "pure" is fully appropriate
here since I count at least 11 prominent translations that use
it. The English word means several things, including faultless,
unadulterated, uncontaminated, undefiled, moral, ethical,
guiltless and sincere. Purity is a desirable quality.

God thought it was good, too. In the Old Testament God
dictated precise and detailed rules for worship. Purity was
stressed over and over in those laws as the Jews were to avoid
being "unclean" and to practice all of the minute details of
purifying themselves at particular intervals in their lives. They
were to wash their hands and feet. They were to avoid contact

with dead bodies or human waste. They were to eat only those foods that God had declared to be pure. The subject of purity permeates at least two complete books of the Old Testament: Exodus and Leviticus. Purity was particularly important to God and to the ceremonies specified for worshiping God.

These rituals were essential because they taught the Jews that purity required personal effort and diligence; that purity did not come naturally. In fact, the natural order of the world was impurity. They would need to work carefully and obediently with great trust in the Father of all purity in order to achieve the purity that God demanded. Vigilance and faithfulness powered by personal faith in the living God were the only way. Purity is good, but it never comes naturally.

The prophet Haggai illustrates this with these words,

"If a person carries consecrated meat in the fold of his garment, and that fold touches some bread or stew, some wine, oil or other food, does it become consecrated?'"
The priests answered, "No."
Then Haggai said, "If a person defiled by contact with a dead body touches one of these things, does it become defiled?"
"Yes," the priests replied, "it becomes defiled" (Haggai 2:12-13 NIV).

Do you see Haggai's point? Clean things don't cleanse what has been contaminated, but corrupt things do pollute the good. Uncleanness is the natural state. Purity comes only through eliminating the impurity by careful attention to God's standards and through abiding faith in God's sustaining strength.

"And chiefly Thou, O Spirit, that dost prefer
Before all temples the upright
heart and pure."
-John Milton

> **Woe to you, teachers of the law and Pharisees,
> you hypocrites! You are like whitewashed
> tombs, which look beautiful on the outside but
> on the inside are full of dead men's bones and
> everything unclean. In the same way, on the
> outside you appear to people as righteous but
> on the inside you are full of
> hypocrisy and wickedness.**
> **Matthew 23:27-28**

But, although the ritual purity of the Old Testament was an expression of God's standard, it had limitations. It did clearly highlight God's standards for purity. It did establish the principle that purity was not natural and must be cultivated with discipline and clear direction and faith in the God who strengthens us for the challenge. It did affirm that purity is achieved only by attention to small details. But, the ritual purity of Exodus and Leviticus fell short in that it dealt primarily with externals when God's first priority is the heart. *"Man looks at the outward appearance, but the LORD looks at the heart"* (1 Samuel 16:7).

Nearly a thousand years later, after Israel had occupied the Promised Land and built the temple and become fully acquainted with ritual purity, God's prophets began to instruct Israel that God wanted their heart to be purified above all. The temple practices were important to God, but only as a symbol and a pattern of what He wanted in their hearts.

- Wash and make yourselves clean. Take your evil deeds out of my sight (Isaiah 1:16).
- Jerusalem, wash the evil from your heart and be saved. How long will you harbor wicked thoughts? (Jeremiah 4:14).
- I will sprinkle clean water on you, and you will be clean; I will cleanse you from all your impurities and from all

your idols. I will give you a new heart and put a new spirit in you; I will remove from you your heart of stone and give you a heart of flesh (Ezekiel 36:25-26).

Finally, the concept of purity as a spiritual washing of our heart and mind, rather than a physical washing of our hands and feet, came to full maturity in the Gospels and Epistles:

> **Woe to you, teachers of the law and Pharisees, you hypocrites! You clean the outside of the cup and dish, but inside they are full of greed and self-indulgence. Blind Pharisee! First clean the inside of the cup and dish, and then the outside also will be clean (Matthew 23:25-26).**

Jesus made it abundantly clear that purity is an internal matter. Soiled pigs can be washed clean, but it does not change their basic instincts. Temple priests could perform every ritual of purity prescribed by the law and still have a heart filled with lust, greed and anger. People can attend church, teach Bible lessons, preach sermons, but if their heart is soiled it is all wrong.

The biblical teaching on purity evolved from the symbolic purity of Exodus and Leviticus, to the combination of ritual and personal purity among the prophets, to the final description of purity as fully a function of the heart. It was all good because it all contributed to unfolding the essential truth that spiritual purity is commanded for those who would be God's people. Purity is good. God wants purity. *Think about what is pure.*

> "God would not rub so hard if it were
> not to fetch out the dirt that is ingrained in
> our natures. God loves purity so well He had
> rather see a hole than a spot in His
> child's garments."
> -William Gurnall

58

Create in me a pure heart, O God.
Psalm 51:10

In 1999, I served as a volunteer pilot with Mission Aviation Fellowship in Mali, West Africa. Our purpose there was to provide aviation services for the missionaries and other aid workers who labored in that poor, remote, desert country.

In order to subsidize the operation we also flew some commercial work, including frequent flights to a large gold mining operation in the desert at a place called Sadiola. Mali has always been a gold producer. In 1433, its famous Emperor Kanku Mussa carried eight tons of gold with him on his pilgrimage to Mecca. There is a legend that Mussa tethered his horse with a single gold nugget. Mali has lots of gold, but the easy stuff was found a long time ago.

Sadiola was an amazing place. It was a complete city built in a remote wilderness for the purpose of extracting gold from an enormous open pit mine. 1500 people lived and worked in that community, which was equipped with schools and housing, an electrical generating station and medical facilities, an impressive store and an airstrip. The mine pit was hundreds of feet deep and perhaps a mile across. You could watch the excavating equipment on the bottom loading the big Caterpillar transporters, which would then trundle up a spiral roadway with tons of dirt to be processed. These were trucks so large that the drivers had to climb a ladder up to their seats. They each carried many tons of dirt and they cycled up and back all day in a chain of vehicles.

One or two days a week, the miners would blast new material from the pit wall using 20,000 pounds of amfo (ammonium nitrate and fuel oil) and creating an explosion that shook buildings and rattled windows a mile or more away.

Eight Stone Gates

That massive volume of dirt from the mine was crushed and washed and passed through a chemical extraction process that separated the gold from all the other material. In order to produce one ounce of gold (about the size of a half-dollar coin) the technicians had to process several tons of dirt. Think of that: tons of dirt for an ounce of gold.

On Fridays, we would fly the gold out to the capital city of Bamako where it was loaded onto an airplane for Brussels. That trip was an Indiana Jones moment, with guys in camo carrying AK-47s and riding in Land Rovers coming in a trail of dust from the processing center to the airstrip. They would then circle the airplane while the gold was loaded and we prepared to leave with one of them aboard as an armed guard.

In a typical week, the mine produced perhaps 1000 kilos of gold, about enough by volume to fill a large suitcase, but worth $30 million on the day this was written. That pure gold had been locked into mountains of dirt so finely dispersed that it was not visible to the eye. In the ground it was useless. Even above ground in piles it was without value. But, when the raw material had been crushed, washed and treated it brought forth pure gold. The gold was there all the time. It just needed to be brought out; and when it was it had great value. Pure is good.

You and I are like that. We have been created in the image of God. If we have surrendered our lives to Him through Christ, we have been given the presence of the Holy Spirit to dwell in us. But while He is certainly there, our raw material must be crushed, washed and treated to bring forth things of purity and value. *Think on pure things.*

"Like the stained cloth that whitens in the
sun, grow pure by being shone upon."
-Thomas Moore

**Since we have these promises, dear friends,
let us purify ourselves from everything that
contaminates body and spirit, perfecting
holiness out of reverence for God.
2 Corinthians 7:1**

So, the challenge is to screen our thoughts so that only those that are pure pass through the gate of our mind. We are besieged by thoughts of all varieties. They assemble at the gates of our mind and struggle for entrance. Without any care on our part they will all gain entrance and many will do damage. The bad will overwhelm the good and become entrenched. They will corrupt, conflict and confuse. *"Bad company corrupts good character"* *(1 Corinthians 15:33).*

John Newton was a man in whom the image of God was so dispersed among the dirt of life that it became invisible. John had never built the mental walls and hung the strong gates that could protect his mind from the corrupt enemy.

John was born in 1725 to an English merchant ship captain. At the age of eleven, he went to sea with his father and after several years joined the crew of a slave ship carrying African slaves to England under horrendous conditions. For a time, he was employed by a slave trader in Sierra Leone, and then he went back to sea as captain of his own slave ship. He later remembered those days as times of being "an infidel and a libertine." There was raw material in John Newton, who was created in God's image, but it was not apparent to anyone. The walls and gates were broken and empty.

In 1748, sailing home aboard the merchant vessel *Greyhound,* John Newton experienced a powerful storm that nearly sank the ship. At that moment of crisis he called out to God as Jonah did in the belly of a whale and found that God was there, was real and was available to any who called. *"Salvation comes from* the LORD" (Jonah 2:9). For the rest of his life John Newton, celebrated that anniversary of March 21st as the day his life changed. He would later express in his famous hymn that it was amazing grace that had caused his heart to fear and that same grace had relieved those fears and saved a wretch named John Newton.

That was the day when John Newton recognized the God of Heaven and Jesus His Son as his new Lord and Savior, and in that clarity of understanding he began to build walls and hang gates that would screen his thoughts. That was the day when John Newton began to exclude the impure, corrupt and base thoughts from his mind. It did not happen in a day, but over time; as the walls were built and the gates were hung, John Newton's mind became the residence of thoughts that were, among other things, pure. Not surprisingly, John Newton went on to become one of the greatest preachers and teachers that England has ever known, first in the small town of Olney and later for 27 years in London. During those years, John Newton teamed with William Wilberforce for 20 years to write and eventually pass legislation that would abolish slavery forever in the British Empire. And during all of those years he produced some of the greatest hymns ever written. *"Amazing grace, how sweet the sound that saved a wretch like me"* were words of powerful and personal meaning to John Newton.

At the end of his life, this wretch of a slaver began to suffer from blindness, confusion and senility. In his last, difficult days he would say to a close friend, *"My memory is nearly gone but I remember two things; that I am a great sinner and that Christ is a great savior."*

Surely that will stand for all time as purity of thought.

"Simplicity reaches out after God; purity
discovers and enjoys Him."
-Thomas a Kempis

**Everyone who has this hope in Him purifies
himself, just as he is pure.
1 John 3:3**

This is not very complicated stuff. Religious ceremony can never make you pure. Good manners will not fumigate the mind. Simple education cannot cleanse your thoughts. Building the walls and hanging the gates can only begin with a clear vision of the purity, holiness and goodness of God. That fear and reverence and awesome respect is the beginning of all wisdom and hope, and that hope is what naturally leads to a desire for purity. If you are convinced that there is gold to be mined, you will be motivated to find it, and if you appeal to the God of all helps, He will empower you.

And among the host of thoughts that clamor at the gates of our minds there is some pure gold. It is dispersed through that crowd of thoughts like gold in the soil of Mali, but if your walls are solid and your gates are well protected, with God's help you can find it and extract it. Think on things in the purity of faith in the Sovereign God; think with humility, forgiveness, kindness, patience and ... you get the idea. *Think on pure things.*

Faith is pure. Faith in God and the atoning work of Jesus is supported by mountains of evidence, but it is still faith. This faith cannot and will not ever be the product of proof because God has made clear that, *"Without faith it is impossible to please Him"* *(Hebrews 11:6).* Proof would undermine the basic relationship of faith and trust.

Faith is not a possession, but an action. It is the conscious and deliberate determination to overrule doubt and proceed on the basis of confidence in the evidence that has been presented, even if it falls short of proof.

Faith is not so mysterious. We place faith in our banks, our universities, our doctors and our spouses. We have no proof, but we consciously set aside our uncertainties because we have serious evidence to do so and move ahead in faith. Without some stabilizing faith in those things we would live in a state of paralyzed indecision and fear about every detail of life.

God loves faith. Not ignorant, blind faith because "Grandma said so" or because "that's what my parents taught me," but faith that is the result of understanding what He has told us in Scripture. *"So faith comes from hearing, and hearing through the word of Christ" (Romans 10:17 ESV).*

Further, He knows that we struggle with this issue of faith. I love that story of a father who by faith brought his convulsing, demon-possessed son to Jesus to ask for healing (Mark 9:17-26). The boy had been frequently thrown into water or fire with imminent risk of death. Jesus asked the man if he really believed that He could accomplish such a miracle. The father who was broken by the stress of a dreadfully afflicted son and desperate for help spoke these simple and honest words, *"I believe; help my unbelief!"* I love that guy. He had sufficient faith to bring his son for healing, but enough humility to see that he needed more. He was able to speak forth a thought of great purity in a moment of severe stress.

Humility is pure. Not some counterfeit that dissembles about how worthless I am. Not some fawning inferiority complex, but a genuine understanding that we are less than we think even though God is able to make us more than we are. Real humility sees my God-given talents and gifts, but sees that they were not given for my personal gratification, but for the glory of God and the help and comfort of others. It is not inconsistent for great men and women of authority and wisdom and brilliance to be men and women of humility. They just see that what they are and what they have is a gift to be used for others. *"Humble yourselves before the Lord, and he will exalt you" (James 4:10).* Humble thoughts are pure thoughts.

Forgiveness is pure—real forgiveness, in which we covenant with God to not remember the wrong done to us even though that "not remembering" may require serious effort to exclude certain thoughts when they recur over and over.

Kindness is pure. Sincere kindness, with nothing expected in return, is pure. Patience is pure. As is gentleness, compassion, self-control and love. Pure is good. God loves purity and especially in our thoughts. *Think on pure things.*

"There is a difference between innocence
and purity. Innocence is the characteristic of
a child; purity is the characteristic of a man
or woman who knows what the tendencies
and temptations to go wrong are and who
has overcome them."
-Oswald Chambers

**Keep yourself pure.
1 Timothy 5:22b**

But there is still more. There are lovely thoughts, admirable thoughts, excellent thoughts and praiseworthy thoughts ...

Eight Stone Gates

Chapter Seven

The Gate of Lovely Thoughts

"Why should we think upon things that are
lovely? Because thinking determines life."
William James

**Have this mind in you, which
was also in Christ Jesus.
Philippians 2:5**

We continue our thinking about walls and gates: Walls that protect our minds from the enemies outside and gates that allow only friends and allies to enter. It is a concept that challenges contemporary thought, which considers all ideas as having value; that no thought should be rejected as invalid; that anything is acceptable because there is no objective standard.

But we are thinking of mental walls and gates because even common sense recognizes that some thoughts are corrupt and destructive. Thoughts of random murder and mayhem, thoughts of violating children and abusing the elderly; thoughts of revenge or deceit or slander or self harm are destructive to the thinker and to society.

There is a standard for healthy and holy thinking. It has been fixed from the beginning of time and it was succinctly stated by Paul as God's representative when he wrote to the church in Philippi, *"whatever is true, whatever is noble, whatever is right, whatever is pure, whatever is lovely, whatever is admirable — if anything is excellent or praiseworthy — think about such things."*

So, after the True, Noble, Right and Pure gates, we come to the next buttress of mental and spiritual construction called the "Lovely Gate."

Eight Stone Gates

The word that Paul uses here is a compound word used only once in the New Testament. Only once. "Prosphiles" builds on the Greek word for "having affection" (philos) by adding the prefix "pros" meaning "toward." Thus, this cobbled together Greek word carries the idea of "movement toward things that are worthy of affection."

"Prosphiles" doesn't translate in a clean and convenient manner, but the English word "lovely" works well in capturing the idea that these are thoughts that stimulate our thinking toward ("pros") a deep and moving affection ("philos") for things that reveal the loveliness and grandeur of a great Creator in the most exquisite manner. Some of these thoughts may be snapshots of the opulence of creation and others may simply be contemplations of some inner beauty of a heart and a life that strive to honor Him. *Think about things that are lovely.*

> "The value of a relationship is in direct proportion to the time that you invest in the relationship."
> - Brian Tracy

Two men owed money to a certain moneylender ... Neither of them had the money to pay him back, so he canceled the debts of both. Now which of them will love him more?
Luke 7:41

The Bible is filled with lovely stories: accounts of human compassion (the Good Samaritan), courage (David vs. Goliath), faith (Abraham), perseverance (Job), loyalty (Ruth) and many more. It is a book filled with stories that move us toward great affection *(prosphiles)* for the people (the heroes and heroines) who lived out Godly principles under difficult circumstances. In that way they are lovely stories. *Think about things that are lovely.*

68

In the Gospel of Luke (7:36-50), there is a lovely story of extravagant affection and reckless giving. The central figure of this story is a woman Luke describes as having lived "a sinful life." Her specific sin is not mentioned, but it is likely to have been prostitution, a particularly grievous offense in the eyes of the Jews, although actually no more offensive to God than my pride or your gossip or someone else's subtle deceit.

She was likely a poor woman, a hard woman, an abused woman and a woman heavily burdened by the weight of her sinful lifestyle prior to meeting Jesus. She was also, presumably, a Gentile; a woman who lived outside the faith of Israel, and in that sense like a woman today who has no church affiliation and who is likely to be antagonistic to the formalities and peculiar culture of church people. And often for good reason. As a prostitute she perhaps had never known love and now she did.

She was not seeking forgiveness, since it is clear from the context that she had already experienced that. She only desired to express her deep appreciation and affection for the One who opened the door to heaven to a woman who had assumed she was locked out; assumed that she was too bad, too sinful, too far gone. She had assumed that the door was shut and barred and she was eternally lost. Except—except for the Redeemer who was in the process of purchasing her with His blood and adopting her into His family.

This woman, this outcast of society, had experienced Jesus as her soul-satisfying treasure through the forgiveness of her sins. She was responding in utter humility and gratitude by sacrificing her only worldly treasure. She had slipped inconspicuously into the gather and, oblivious to the gasps of witnesses, quietly emptied an alabaster box of precious ointment onto the feet of Jesus.

Because of her adoration this previously wounded and sin-sick woman desired to express her affection in some public way. Further, she was moved to express her love with reckless abandon, which she did in the presence of a considerable audience who were dining together in a prominent citizen's home.

We see three things in the actions of this woman: First is her sacrifice, seen in her purchase of expensive perfume. The jar of perfume she emptied on Jesus' feet would have been bought at very high cost; possibly weeks or months of an average wage. This blemished woman's action was an audacious, extravagant gesture of affection for the One Who had given her eternal life.

Second, we note that her gesture of affection was flagrant in its disregard of rigid social and religious customs. She didn't care that women were not supposed to let down their hair in public or touch a man. She was not interested in conventions. This wounded, rejected, hurt woman was only interested in expressing her devotion to the One who had healed her soul and called her His friend, wanting nothing in return but affection and loyalty. He was completely unlike the people who had used her for years. So, after she poured the perfume out, she wet his feet with her tears and wiped them with her hair. Weeping and wiping, wiping and weeping, and loving because this was the One worthy of extravagant love.

And why was she weeping? Because her sin was forgiven; and because her sin was still a dark memory of her past broken life. Because she could see both: where she had been and where she was. It was gratitude mixed with memory, like a cancer survivor who weeps at the news of her healing with vivid memories of that terrible disease.

Finally, we see that it is in every respect a lovely story; a story that is capable of moving our thoughts toward great affection. It is a story of the Savior and the saved and the love between them expressed by each in the form of extravagant sacrifice. Her perfume. His blood.

It is eternally lovely. It is a lovely thought to meditate on the love of God, His mercy, my forgiven sin and the love that binds sinners with the Savior. I wish I had the hair to wipe His feet, but that is another story. *Think about things that are lovely.*

"This is my Father's world, and to my listening
ears all nature sings, and round me rings
the music of the spheres."
-Maltbie Babcock

**The heavens declare the glory of God;
the skies proclaim the work of his hands.
Psalm 19:1**

God's glory is established forever. He radiates glory spiritually and physically, in power and wisdom, in knowledge and goodness. He is surrounded by glory. He is the very essence of glory. Those who encircle His throne in heaven cry out day and night "Holy, Holy, Holy," not because they are obligated, but because they are overcome and obsessed with the magnificence of His glory and can do nothing else. It is a thing of inconceivable loveliness.

We mortals can only see that glory in small particulars. We see it in the manifestation of God's Holy Spirit when his people are motivated to kindness and gentleness and mercy; to forgiveness and self-sacrifice and humility. We see it, also, in endless dimensions of His creation. There are innumerable examples of God's glory, but for a few moments consider the atmosphere. The skies do proclaim the work of His hands, as you know if you have savored the grandeur of the stars and planets on a clear night. But that "second heaven" is just one part of the skies that proclaim His glory.

Eight Stone Gates

The wonder of the atmosphere, "the first heaven," and its chemical composition that is perfect for human and other life is expressed in a myriad of lovely sights. One that is particularly lovely to me is called "The Glory."

Originally, "The Glory" was called "The Specter of Brocken," after a mountain by that name in the Hartz Mountains of Germany. Climbers noticed that when the mountain's top was shrouded in light fog, they would sometimes see a dark phantom—a specter—surrounded by a circle of rainbow in the distance. Eventually they realized that this vision was merely their own shadow cast into the fog with an enchanting, perfect circle of rainbow that made it both unusual and beautiful.

Aviators often see this phenomenon when flying toward a cloud with the sun behind them and they call this "The Glory." As the airplane approaches the cloud with the sun behind it, they see a perfect circle of rainbow surrounding the airplane's shadow. From a distance it is all faint. As the cloud grows closer the shadow increases in size and the rainbow builds intensity until there is a single moment—a brief flash—when the airplane shadow is large and dark, the rainbow is bright and vivid just before the airplane is swallowed by "The Glory" and it is gone. The darkness is swallowed by light.

Piercing The Glory is, well, glorious. It is a thing that moves us toward great affection (*prosphiles*) for God's amazing creative power. It is truly lovely. The memory of that experience is a thought worthy of entrance through the Lovely Gate, not just because of the eye-watering artistic beauty, but because of the God who created such dynamic beauty, not to mention the image of my black sin being swallowed by the flashing glory of a mighty God. *Think about things that are lovely.*

"Whatever makes an impression on the
heart seems lovely in the eye."
-Sa'Di

**The LORD does not look at the things man
looks at. Man looks at the outward appearance,
but the LORD looks at the heart.
1 Samuel 16:7**

We live in a world that is powerfully focused on the obvious
and external. Loveliness is routinely defined by what can be
seen and felt both physically and emotionally, but there is an
inner loveliness that is uncommon and often unseen. There is
an inner beauty that is not immediately lovely on the surface,
but is extraordinarily compelling when it is discovered. Think
of *The Hunchback of Notre Dame*, or the Beast in *Beauty and the
Beast*.

The Hunchback (Quasimodo) was hideously deformed and
perpetually ridiculed for his ugliness. He was confined to the
cathedral of Notre Dame where he worked as the bell ringer.
He was a man feared for his grotesque ugliness and fearsome
strength, but also a man capable of great and sacrificial love for
a woman unjustly condemned to death. Quasimodo was not
what he appeared to be. His heart was lovely.

In 1674, a boy was born in Southampton, England to a devout,
Christian school teacher and his wife. This boy displayed early
talent as a poetic genius with a deep love and understanding of
the Gospel. He was a prodigy of lovely words and thoughts,
but as he grew his body developed in unattractive ways. As an
adult he was only five feet tall with a huge head that was far too
large for his frail body. His nose was crooked. His eyes were
small. His skin was yellow. His health was consistently poor.
There was nothing physically appealing about Isaac Watts. He
fell in love with a young woman and proposed marriage, but

she refused him and said, "I love the jewel but not the setting." He never married. He lived out his life on the estate of a sympathetic friend.

Isaac Watts had no external beauty, but he had an inner loveliness that prompted him to write over 600 hymns of such poetic splendor that many are commonly sung today after 300 years. Behind the deformed body and the sallow skin was a lovely person made manifest in the words of his wonderful songs.

Quasimodo, the Beast and Isaac Watts each possessed a quality of inner loveliness that the casual observer would miss. It causes me to wonder what I have missed. What inner beauty have I overlooked by focusing on unattractive exteriors? *Think about things that are lovely. Truly lovely.*

> "All the beautiful sentiments in the world
> weigh less than a single lovely action."
> -James Russell Lowell

> **And if anyone gives even a cup of cold water
> to one of these little ones because he is my
> disciple, I tell you the truth, he will
> certainly not lose his reward.
> Matthew 10:42**

Sometimes lovely is common like the beauty of creation, or more intense and complex like a broken prostitute delivered from herself, or deeply moving like faith and creativity in the face of personal adversity. Lovely is whatever draws us into that sense of *prosphiles,* of being drawn toward something worthy of a strong sense of affection; something that reveals the loveliness and magnificence of a great Creator. When God looks at the redeemed, He sees the loveliness of Jesus.

Sometimes it is a simple act of random kindness.

Years ago, I was meeting one of my military friends in a bistro in some foreign port. He showed me a pair of socks he had just bought in the local market. They were excellent, hand-knit, wool socks well suited for the cold weather flying we often were called to do. When a young street boy came in looking for a few coins Bernie gave him some … and the socks. And then we watched as the boy walked outside and gave one sock to his brother. One sock. One sock for each brother. Even one sock can be lovely.

The Lovely Gate is where we admit thoughts that draw us into that deep affection and wonder *(prosphiles)* for the objects and actions themselves and even more so for the God who created them.

Think about things that are lovely. Think about things that move you toward God with deep affections. But don't stop here. We should also think about things that are admirable.

> "A Christmas candle is a lovely thing;
> It makes no noise at all,
> But softly gives itself away."
> -Eva Logue

**On the glorious splendor of your majesty,
and on your wondrous works, I will meditate.
Psalm 145:5 (ESV)**

Eight Stone Gates

Chapter Eight

The Gate of Admirable Thoughts

"Men value things in three ways: as useful,
as pleasant or sources of pleasure, and as ...
intrinsically admirable or honorable."
-Mortimer Adler

**Whatever is admirable ... think
about such things.
Philippians 4:8**

Sometimes people ask, "Hey, what are you thinking?" You think about your finances, your relationships, your past hurts, your fears and anxieties, your career, your favorite sports team, your reputation, your parents and children and spouse, your responsibilities and a host of major and minor thoughts that may or may not be admirable. But, when you think about it, what do you think about?

In that one verse numbered Philippians 4:8, Paul lists eight categories of thought to strive for. One of those, the sixth one, is another cobbled-together Greek word used only this one place in the Bible, although it is common in other Greek writing. The word is a combination of the Greek *"eu"* meaning "good" or "well" and the word *"pheme"* which can be translated "report."

In the English language we use a nearly identical word (euphemism) to describe an agreeable or inoffensive expression that is used in place of one that may sound harsh or unpleasant. We describe used automobiles as "pre-owned." We never say someone is old; they are "mature' or "golden aged." People don't just die, they "fail to fulfill their wellness potential." Euphemisms are "good sayings" or "agreeable expressions" in place of something more harsh or unpleasant. But in English, these euphemisms are a distortion of the truth for the purpose of avoiding unpleasantness or offense. They are an attempt to disguise the true meaning, whereas the Greek "euphemos," as used in Philippians 4:8, is a straightforward expression with a pretty clear definition.

Bible translators have used several English words or combinations to grasp the concept of the Greek word "euphemos" including "good report," "commendable," "good repute," "gracious" and "admirable." Any one of them works well but since we began with a translation that chose "admirable," let's just stick with that.

Admirable. Think about things that are admirable; commendable; worth talking about. And, incidentally, worth thinking about. *Whatever is admirable — think about such things.*

> "We are willing to be pleased
> but we are not willing to admire."
> -Samuel Johnson

I will sacrifice a freewill offering to you;
I will praise your name, O LORD, for it is good.
Psalm 54:6

We are thinking of things that are admirable; things that have such character and quality that they are worth talking about, thinking about and spreading around; things that are commendable. It is good to have a memory file of such things because when cruel and nasty thoughts gather at the walls of our mind we can filter them out by opening the gate of admirable thoughts.

There are many admirable qualities we can remember and savor, but one of those is the thought of people who have demonstrated self-sacrifice, genuine self-denial. It is an admirable thought because our natural bent is to think about ourselves and serve ourselves; so those examples of people who break out of that trap and think about and serve others are admirable.

One day during Jesus' ministry, He sat down opposite the treasury of the temple where people came to drop off their financial offerings. In this court of the temple there were 13 metal chests for charitable contributions. These chests were narrow at the mouth and wide at the bottom so they were sometimes referred to as "trumpets." They weren't really trumpets and they didn't sound like trumpets, they just looked something like trumpets and so the people thought of them that way.

But in a unique way, they could be made to function like a trumpet in announcing an offering. If you dropped in a handful of large coins these treasury chests would resound with a satisfying clang, which broadcast to everyone nearby that you were a big giver. If you had only a small coin to drop, the sound would be negligible and you would have no public recognition for your little offering no matter how sacrificial. Surely this appealed to base human nature, which so loves recognition, and people would have enjoyed dropping their sizable donations with a satisfying and public jangle. You could cash your $10 bill for 40 quarters and look good.

On this particular day, Jesus observed several rich people drop in their offerings; presumably these were large collections of big coins and made a very public sound. How nice to be publicly acknowledged as a big spender for God. Everyone loves a big giver.

Then there came a poor widow who threw in two "mites," the smallest coin then in circulation. Mites were crude, copper coins, roughly minted with irregular edges and about ½ inch in diameter, or about the size of a US dime. Mites were definitely not designed to impress anyone with their resonance from the "trumpets." We do know that Jesus heard them, but it is unlikely that anyone else in that temple court heard the sound of those two miniature coins dropping into the offering box.

And yet there was a stunning consequence to this small offering, which became one of history's most important and publicized financial transactions. The creator of the universe heard those mites fall into the "trumpet" above the racket of much larger offerings. He not only heard them, He commented on them in a way that assured they would be part of the eternal record of God's revelation to mankind and an admirable example for countless generations.

And there was a heavenly reason for this consequence. The widow in this story gave all out of proportion to her wealth. This was a truly sacrificial gift. It came out of her immediate needs and not her surplus. It is likely that she returned home to a night of hunger and a future of uncertainty because she had given everything she owned. There was no more. She had only two mites. She gave two mites.

The point that Jesus makes here is that the gift which counts is the gift which costs and this widow's gift—a woman without other support, a woman alone—cost everything.

Think of the reasonable justifications this widow could have employed: "My pennies aren't enough to help anyone. Let all those who can afford it give. I need this for my supper."

In the end, she understood that giving is not so much about providing for someone else as it is about denying our self. I need to give wisely, but I need to give because I need to practice self-denial and the rest will take care of itself.

This fragile widow's gift was truly admirable, as are the many sacrificial acts of self-denial that we hear about from time to time. Think about those you know who give their time and talents. Think about those who plant their young families in strange and difficult places so that they can minister to other, poorer people. Think about things that are admirable.

"Perseverance is not a long race; it is many
short races one after the other."
-Walter Elliot

**As you know, we consider blessed
those who have persevered.
James 5:11**

We are considering the gate to our mind through which we admit thoughts of admirable things. We are attacked frequently and regularly with wrong, evil, selfish, bitter, angry thoughts and our only defense is to build walls around our thinking that have eight gates to admit good thoughts; thoughts that are true, noble, right, pure, lovely, admirable, ... and more. Let's look at some admirable attributes ...

Perseverance and patience are admirable attributes; related but different. Patience is passive. Patience sits and waits, trusting God for His wisdom and goodness. Jeremiah said it like this, *"I say to myself, 'The Lord is my portion; therefore I will wait for him'"(Lamentations 3:24).* This kind of patience is certainly admirable, but it is just the fraternal twin of perseverance.

Perseverance, on the other hand, is the active management of life's business in the face of obstacles. While we wait with patience for God's answer to prayer we can actively go about the normal affairs of life. Both patience and perseverance are admirable qualities, but perseverance in the face of great adversity seems especially so.

Eight Stone Gates

"Consider the postage stamp, my son.
It secures success through its ability to stick
to one thing until it gets there."
-Josh Billings

**Therefore, since we are surrounded by such
a great cloud of witnesses, let us throw off
everything that hinders and the sin that
so easily entangles, and let us run with
perseverance the race marked out for us.
Hebrews 12:1**

Glenn Cunningham was born to a hard-working family in the farming town of Everetts, Kansas in 1909. By the age of six, Glenn was contributing to the family income by walking the two miles to school in the early morning with his nine year old brother, Floyd, to start the fire in the schoolhouse stove. It was a simple chore with a small compensation, but every bit helped.

One cold morning in February of 1916 the boys completed their usual task of loading the stove with wood and then drizzling on some kerosene to jump-start the fire. On this particular morning when Floyd dropped the match into the stove it flared with an explosive force that engulfed the boys in a sheet of flame. Someone had filled the kerosene can with gasoline.

Floyd was so badly burned that he lived for only a few minutes. Glenn was taken to the hospital with devastating burns to his entire lower body. At first the doctors thought he would not live and then they thought his legs should be amputated because he surely would not walk again. He had lost all of the toes on his left foot; the transverse arch was seriously and permanently damaged; the flesh of that leg had been eaten away and the right leg was misshapen and two inches shorter than the left. Surely he was destined for life as a cripple. He was six years old.

The doctors recommended stretching therapy for the legs and Glenn was so determined that when his father tired of stretching his legs he would ask his mother to continue, and when she tired he would do all he could by himself. It was excruciatingly painful. He was seven years old.

One day, his mother pushed him out to the back yard in his wheelchair and was amazed to see him crawl out of his chair, pull himself up by the back fence and force his legs to move. He then did this same thing every day for weeks until he had worn a path along the fence from his awkward walking. He was ten.

Over a period of months, his legs started to function again, but he discovered something unusual. It hurt to walk, but not to run. So, he ran everywhere. Within two years he was the fastest runner in town. He was twelve.

In high school, Glenn continued to run and in his last high school race set a national one-mile record of 4 minutes 24.7 seconds. He was 17.

At the University of Kansas, Glenn set numerous records in the mile, half mile, 1500 meter and 800 meter. In 1932, he ran the fastest outdoor mile ever run, anywhere. He won two NCAA titles and eight AAU championships. But he wasn't finished with life and perseverance.

He earned a doctorate in physical education and then served two years in the Navy during WWII. During his running career, he shrewdly saved and invested his earnings with which he purchased two large ranches. On one of them, he later operated a home for troubled youth, eventually helping over 9,000 underprivileged kids at his Glenn Cunningham Ranch.

All of his life, Glenn Cunningham admired perseverance. He is quoted as saying, "If you stay in the running, if you have endurance, you are bound to win over those who don't."

His favorite Bible verse, the one that sustained him through years of perseverance and which he shared with countless troubled youth, was Isaiah 40:31: *"but those who hope in the Lord will renew their strength. They will soar on wings like eagles; they will run and not grow weary, they will walk and not be faint."*

Perseverance is a wonderful and admirable quality. Glenn Cunningham set a high standard for perseverance in his life in many dimensions, but we can persevere in the lesser crises of our life through simple faith and trust in a loving God. And when the enemy gathers at the walls with thoughts of anger and bitterness and lust, unforgiveness, discouragement or envy, we can exclude those outlaws and admit thoughts that are admirable. *Think about what is admirable.*

> "This is the mark of a really admirable man:
> steadfastness in the face of trouble."
> -Ludwig van Beethoven

> **For it is commendable if a man bears up**
> **under the pain of unjust suffering because**
> **he is conscious of God.**
> **But how is it to your credit if you receive a**
> **beating for doing wrong and endure it? But if**
> **you suffer for doing good and you endure it,**
> **this is commendable before God.**
> **1 Peter 2:19-20**

Shadrach, Meshach and Abednego were certainly admirable in response to the proud and pagan demands of King Nebuchadnezzar II of Babylon. Think about it.

These three young captive exiles from Israel, living in the enemy's capital of Babylon, along with their friend Daniel, were probably orphans. Apparently they had all found favor at Nebuchadnezzar's court and were being specially schooled for administrative work. These were the brightest and the best of Israel and, considering that they were exiles and captives, they had particularly favorable prospects in the Babylonian government. If they stayed on this career track they would live in the comfort of the royal staff.

Sometime during this period, Nebuchadnezzar had a monument built that soared 90 feet into the air. It is not entirely clear what the monument, was but think of a great stone pedestal supporting a massive statue covered in gold. This grandiose monument was most likely dedicated to the god Nebu, whose name forms the first two syllables of Nebuchadnezzar's name. It may have been an image of the king himself. Undoubtedly there was some link between the statue and the king, inspired by his grandiose thoughts of personal divinity.

On the day of dedication for this monument, all the government officials were gathered, from the king's closest advisors down through the next seven levels of bureaucratic administration. Everybody who was anyone in Babylon was there. Apparently, from the story, Shadrach, Meshach and Abednego were there also.

During this dedication ceremony it was decreed that when the band played everyone in sight was to fall on their face and worship the statue. Not just honor, but worship, venerate and exalt. They were to accept this lump of stone and gold as a god. It was an abomination to Shadrach, Meshach and Abednego, who believed in one true God, Jehovah. They were unwilling to worship a pagan image and they were unwilling to pretend.

So, the band played. The crowd fell on their faces. The boys remained conspicuously standing. It was a courageous move for young men in a foreign country and it led to a death sentence.

Nebuchadnezzar decreed that they be burned alive in a furnace so hot that the attendants died in the process of throwing in the young men. In the end, their God—the only true God—protected them and they survived, but only after they had committed their lives completely to His care, not knowing the immediate outcome.

They had accepted persecution, punishment and certain death for an act that was glorifying to God. They were unjustly condemned and harassed. They never recanted. They suffered for doing good. They were men of integrity and men of God, worthy of serious admiration. *Think about what is admirable.*

It is one more in God's list of eight fruitful topics for thought. Think about things that are *euphemos,* things that are good to report.

In the midst of the battle for the mind there are always admirable things to recall as a means of excluding corrupting thoughts. There are memories and stories of courage, diligence, honesty, perseverance, sacrifice and service. The world is filled with depressing and distressing thoughts, but in the midst of that there is much that is admirable to think about. Think about what is admirable that you may live an admirable life bringing glory to God at every opportunity.

"Admiration is one of the most bewitching,
enthusiastic passions of the mind."
-William Warburton

**Then I commanded the Levites to purify
themselves and go and guard the gates.
Nehemiah 13:22**

Chapter Nine

The Gate of Excellent Thoughts

"The secret of living a life of excellence
is merely a matter of thinking thoughts
of excellence. Really, it's a matter of
programming our minds with the kind of
information that will set us free."
-Charles R. Swindoll

**If anything is excellent ... think
about such things.
Philippians 4:8** (partial)

In a Greek/Roman world pervaded by much coarse and immoral thought, much like our own, the apostle Paul wrote a piece of Godly and God-inspired advice to the little church in Philippi. The people there may have lived in a different millennium, but they struggled with their own set of corrosive thoughts; thoughts about pagan gods, church contention, rigid and prideful personal opinions, marital bitterness, financial woes, oppressive and corrupt governments, and all manner of potential catastrophes. And their heads surely swirled with thoughts of the neighbor's wife, their relative's immoralities, and their spouse's failures.

In this stew of corrupt thinking, Paul advised them to concentrate on eight righteous topics, "whatever is true, noble, right, pure, lovely, admirable, excellent ... think about these things." Good advice. *Think about things that are excellent.*

The Greek that Paul used here ("arête") is a word that has a very wide meaning, but essentially focuses on the excellence of a person. It was a favorite word of the times, often used to describe "virtue" as it was defined in heathen circles. In those contexts, it has a sort of earthy and human meaning for virtue (think of Superman or John Wayne) and that is probably why it is used only once by Paul and twice by Peter in the New Testament.

In the spiritual sense implied here, "arête" is the excellence that leads people to moral virtue (humility, modesty, purity, etc.), but it conveys a robust and vigorous form of such virtue. This is no wimpy, passive "niceness"; it is a dynamic virtue applied to very real circumstances of life. Peter uses this word to describe God's personal virtue as well as the standard of excellence that we believers are called to. (1 Peter 2:9; 2 Peter 1:3,5). So, we come full circle and consider the meaning to be excellence of virtue. *Think about what is excellent.*

"I assure you that I would rather excel others
in the knowledge of what is excellent, than in
the extent of my power and dominion."
-Plutarch

**Now for this very reason also, applying all
diligence, in your faith supply moral excellence,
and in your moral excellence, knowledge.
2 Peter 1:5 (NASB)**

There is no stronger example of moral excellence than the act of forgiveness. It is our very nature to seek revenge, to get even, to hit back. It is woven into our very DNA so that when we are insulted or abused the first instinct of the human heart is to seek revenge. The problem is that revenge only succeeds in converting a perceived personal "right" into a great wrong.

One problem with forgiveness is that it is so poorly understood. It is not overlooking or forgetting or ignoring. Godly forgiveness—the forgiveness that God extends to those who believe—is to not remember.

Not remember … That requires some careful thought, but since we are thinking about thinking, what could be more appropriate?

God has promised multiple times in Scripture that He would not remember our confessed sin. He never said that He would forget. He said that He would not remember and there is a great distinction. "Forget" would mean something like deleting the file as we do on a computer. It would be gone and unavailable and inaccessible and unable to cause any further distress. That would be nice, but God cannot do that because it would contradict that part of His basic nature which is omniscience.

There is nothing He cannot do and there is nothing He cannot know, including His awareness of all our sins and transgressions, past, present and future. He knows. He cannot forget. But, when we confess those sins He promises (covenants) to never remember them. And since he commands us (not suggests, but commands, Colossians 3:13), to forgive as He forgives we are stuck with this definition of forgiveness which is to "not remember." It is His model for us. Biblical forgiveness means, by definition, "not remembering."

This is hard spiritual labor. Not remembering means coping with the insidious attacks of memory that would bring the offense to mind over and over. It means taking control of our thoughts with the personal discipline necessary to avoid talking about the forgiven offense, to pass up any opportunity to remind the offender of the offense or to allow it to interfere with our relationship. It is tough. It was tough for Jesus, who sweat blood in the Garden of Gethsemane at the very thought of enduring the physical and spiritual pain required to forgive us. And it is tough for us, but it is a thing of excellence.

"Forgiveness is the fragrance that the violet
sheds on the heel that has crushed it."
-Mark Twain

Eight Stone Gates

**Their sins and lawless acts I will
remember no more.
Hebrews 10:17**

Jacob DeShazer was born in 1912 in a small town in Oregon. He enlisted in the United States Army Air Corps in 1940 and rose to the rank of Sergeant in his military specialty as a bombardier.

Shortly after the Pearl Harbor attack on December 7th, 1941, Jacob volunteered to join an elite group that would be trained to fly Air Corps bombers from the deck of a Navy Aircraft Carrier to strike Japan. It was a radical and dangerous assignment under the command of one of America's greatest aviators and finest military leaders, Jimmy Doolittle. The raid would ever after be known as the "Doolittle Raid."

This elite group of sixteen select crews trained extensively for three months in Florida and then boarded the USS Hornet for transport to a spot in the Pacific from which they could reach Japan, drop their bombs and then fly on to safety in China.

As the Hornet neared Japan it was spotted by a Japanese communications trawler and the raid was launched earlier than planned to minimize any countermeasures by the Japanese. Because of that early launch they did not have enough fuel to reach their planned destination and DeShazer and the rest of his crew were forced to bail out over Japanese held territory in China. He was captured the next day.

During his captivity he was shipped to Tokyo and held in a series of POW camps for 40 months, 34 of them in solitary confinement. He was repeatedly beaten and starved while three members of his crew were executed and one died of malnourishment. At the war's end Jacob had been returned to a POW camp in China and was eventually liberated by American paratroopers. Jacob had every human right to be a bitter and angry man. He had been unjustly, illegally and inhumanely treated. Jacob should have been resentful and hateful, except …

Except that during his captivity he was given access to a Bible for three weeks. Only three weeks. But during those 21 days he recognized the incredible forgiveness that God offers each of us and resolved to do something with that if he survived. The verse that changed Jacob's life was from Luke 23:34, *"Father, forgive them for they know not what they do."*

After the war, Jacob entered Seattle Pacific College to prepare himself for mission work and then returned to Japan with his wife, Florence, in 1948. Jacob had been beaten, starved and abused by the Japanese people, but the call to forgiveness was stronger than any impulse to hostility and prejudice. Jacob came to see his captors as prisoners of another kind: prisoners of their own ignorance and false religion; prisoners of their sin and anger and discouragement; prisoners of defeat and disillusionment. Jacob had been a prisoner both physically and spiritually, but his compassion surpassed his personal hurt. He was a living paradigm of true forgiveness. *"Father, forgive them for they didn't know what they were doing."*

Think about what is excellent.

When Jacob arrived back in Japan the Japanese people related to his presence with eager questions. "What happened to you? Why did you come back? Didn't they hit you and spit on you and treat you meanly? Why did you want to come back here?"

Before he left for Japan, Jacob penned a tract with the title "I was a Prisoner of Japan" in which he described his reasons for returning. He chronicled his imprisonment and his conversion with a particular focus on Romans 10:9, *"That if you confess with your mouth, 'Jesus is Lord,' and believe in your heart that God raised him from the dead, you will be saved."* It was an evangelical tract that used Jacob's personal experiences as a means of attracting Japanese readers to personal salvation by grace, through faith in Christ. One reader of that tract was an embittered ex-Japanese naval pilot, Mitsuo Fuchida.

> "Forgiveness is the answer to the child's
> dream of a miracle by which what is
> broken is made whole again, what is
> soiled is made clean."
> -Dag Hammarskjold

**Forgive whatever grievances you may
have against one another. Forgive as
the Lord forgave you.
Colossians 3:13b**

Fuchida had been a Captain in the Imperial Japanese Navy Air Service and had personally planned and led the attack on Pearl Harbor on December 7, 1941. He was later wounded at the battle of Midway and survived the war. After the war he was called to testify at some of the war crimes trials against other Japanese officers. This angered Fuchida because he believed the Japanese had acted no differently than the Americans. He thought the trials were nothing more than a victor's revenge, and for that and much more he was bitter.

In the spring of 1947, Fuchida went to Uraga Harbor near Yokosuka to meet a group of returning Japanese prisoners of war. He was amazed to find his former flight engineer, Kazuo Kanegasaki, who he thought had died in the Battle of Midway. When questioned, Kanegasaki told Fuchida that Japanese prisoners were not tortured or abused by the Americans, much to Fuchida's surprise. His former friend and crewmate went on to tell Fuchida of a young lady who served them with the deepest love and respect, but whose parents, missionaries, had been killed by Japanese soldiers on the island of Panay in the Philippines. This concept was inexplicable for Fuchida because under the military Bushido code, revenge was not only permitted it was required. The murder of one's parents would demand a lifetime commitment to retribution in order to restore honor. He became obsessed with understanding why anyone would treat their oppressors with love and forgiveness. It simply did not fit in Fuchida's world view.

In the fall of 1948, Fuchida was in the Shibuya railroad station where someone handed him a copy of Jacob DeShazer's pamphlet, which, in turn, prompted him to buy a Bible. In the Bible, he recognized why that young lady had forgiven her enemies and within a year he became a Christian. In May of 1950, the two airmen met; one who had bombed Pearl Harbor and the other who had bombed Tokyo. One who had been beaten and starved by the Japanese and the other who had been wounded by the Americans in a major battle. Now brothers in Christ, and life-long friends and fellow evangelists, Fuchida later wrote a book titled, "From Pearl Harbor to Golgotha."

And just what is excellent about this story? It is forgiveness. It is the personal and courageous commitment to "not remember" past grievances. It is the determination to love an enemy. It is a thing of towering excellence.

Think about what is excellent.

> "An excellent plumber is infinitely more
> admirable than an incompetent philosopher.
> The society which scorns excellence in
> plumbing because plumbing is a humble
> activity and tolerates shoddiness in
> philosophy because it is an exalted activity
> will have neither good plumbing nor good
> philosophy. Neither its pipes nor
> its theories will hold water."
> -John W. Gardner

**And now I will show you the most excellent way.
1 Corinthians 12:31**

That excellent way that Paul refers to in 1 Corinthians 12:31 is the core message of one of the most excellent of all God's gifts. It is that old black book that sits on your night stand or on the coffee table or, hopefully not, packed in a box in the garage. It is not just the best selling book of all times; it has delivered the wisdom to create democracies, establish common law, define forgiveness, settle disputes, train children, restore marriages, organize personal and business finances and, not incidentally, to save souls, by grace. Truly, that is excellent.

Just as you can't succeed at your profession without careful training, or appreciate the universe without watching the night sky, you cannot value this unique and divine book without devoting some time and energy to reading it. The loveliness is there. The wisdom, poetry, history, hope and grace are all included in even the cheapest copy of the Bible, but it must be mined like gold from a quarry.

Forget that your college professor assured you that it was a myth; forget that your father used it as an instrument of abuse; forget that your peer group considers it irrelevant. None of those opinions change the truth that this is a volume of God's grace presenting the clear words of eternal life. I know it sounds preposterous to some. It did to me until I went to the quarry myself and there I found it was lovely. And still do.

In this book you will find a coherent description of basic human nature. It consistently describes us as inherently self-centered, but capable of great deeds. It faithfully describes the heroes and champions it portrays as flawed even in their excellence: Jacob was a liar and deceiver; Moses was a murderer and a man with a volatile temper; David was an adulterer and murderer; Peter acted like a wimp. This is not a book of cheap, plastic heroes. This is a book that describes the frailty and the capacity of human nature without literary distortion.

In this book you will find excellent history beyond what you learned at your high school or university. It is not a complete history, and much of the biblical history is unknown from other sources, but over 6000 major archeological discoveries have only substantiated the biblical account. None have produced seriously conflicting evidence.

In this book you will find a thoroughly unique solution to your guilt and shame. You will find that you cannot perform your way to righteousness, but that you can have righteousness in God's eyes as a gift. You cannot earn eternal glory, but you can have forgiveness and eternal life as a pure and free gift because Jesus Christ paid the penalty. You will find that all of this is true only for those who are serious about a life commitment.

And, in this book you will find hope for today and hope for eternity because those who have made that life commitment actually become the adopted children of God. It is not reasonable. It is not logical. It is not even fair, but it just is. Who said that God's logic must conform to ours?

"Excellent things are rare."
-Plato

Think about what is excellent.
Philippians 4:8 (paraphrase)

Excellent things are indeed rare. Things that have the dynamic, aggressive virtue described by the Greek "arête" have always been rare, but they are worth discovering and they are worth thinking about. In a world saturated with media of all kinds, we are barraged with thoughts of pride, revenge, lust, greed, prejudice, selfishness and more. These thoughts surround the walls of our mind and clamor for entry. They build siege mounds and use battering rams to break the walls, but our business is to strengthen the walls and selectively admit only those thoughts which measure up to the high standards of truth, nobility, purity, loveliness, admirableness, excellence and praiseworthiness.

"Mediocrity is never God's will for us. He calls us to excellence and challenges us to be more than we thought."
-Max Browning

I want you to stress these things, so that those who have trusted in God may be careful to devote themselves to doing what is good. These things are excellent and profitable for everyone.
Titus 3:5

His divine power has given us everything we need for life and godliness through our knowledge of him who called us by his own glory and (excellent) goodness.
2 Peter 1:3

Chapter Ten

The Gate of Praiseworthy Thoughts

"We participate, in a sense, in noble deeds
when we praise them sincerely."
-LaRouchefoucauld

**We will not hide them from their children;
we will tell the next generation
the praiseworthy deeds of the LORD.
Psalm 78:4**

So, we come to the eighth and last category of thought that Paul advises in this single verse we are tracing from Philippians 4:8. Using our metaphor of gates mounted in a stone wall, this is the last doorway to be erected and fortified. This is the gate that admits only those thoughts of things that are praiseworthy, commendable, or worthy of compliment.

All of these conflict with the secular concept of free thinking or declaring all thoughts to be equally valid. If you build your morality on a foundation of nothing but reason and secular education that might be true. Paul, however, was describing the kind of thinking that would logically follow belief in a Holy God and a personal desire to please Him. Paul is not interested in philosophy here; he is not concerned with academic arguments; he is concerned with wisdom and how that wisdom would play out in the minds of those who have a desire to please the God who cares for them.

In an earlier passage, Paul said, *"For the message of the cross is foolishness to those who are perishing, but to us who are being saved it is the power of God. For it is written: 'I will destroy the wisdom of the wise; the intelligence of the intelligent I will frustrate'"* (1 Corinthians 1:18-19).

One piece of "intelligence" that God (through Paul) sets out to frustrate is the idea that our minds can be profitably subjected to any and all thoughts. Everywhere in Scripture it is assumed that some thoughts are simply corrosive and damaging and should be diligently excluded from our thinking. Bitter thoughts, hateful thoughts, selfish thoughts, violent thoughts, and much more, have no place in the mind of a Christian and should be carefully filtered out through those eight gates described in our theme verse of Philippians 4:8: *"Whatever is true, noble, right, pure, lovely, admirable, excellent or praiseworthy, think about such things."*

Think about what is praiseworthy.

> "While it is well enough to leave footprints
> on the sands of time, it is even more
> important to make sure they point in a
> commendable direction."
> -James Branch Cabell

> **These (trials) have come so that your faith—**
> **may be proved genuine and may result in praise,**
> **glory and honor when Jesus Christ is revealed.**
> **1 Peter 1:7**

Personal acts of courage for the sake of others are always praiseworthy. History is filled with acts of cowardice and weakness, greed and pride, power and cruelty, but also with acts of great bravery. Some of those acts of sacrificial valor actually turned the tide of history. These are always worthy of praise.

One of the core elements of Roman culture was the brutal and bloody practice of the gladiator games. Rome commonly sanctioned bloody violence as retribution for enemies, as legal punishment for criminals and as pure entertainment for the masses. Death by crucifixion, wild beasts, burning alive, beheading or being dragged to death by wild horses were common public spectacles and the Roman people came to like them and demand them. In order to supply a constant display of public violence they evolved the gladiatorial games, in which dedicated athletes fought each other or some other hapless victim to a bloody death. It was a public sport viewed by as many as 80,000 people at a time in the coliseum. Trained men would fight captured enemies, wild animals or each other to the death as Roman spectators cheered and wagered on who would survive. The winners were often gravely wounded and losers were dead. It was an appalling spectacle of blood-drenched violence. Historians estimate that 500,000 people and over a million wild animals died gory and violent deaths as a form of public entertainment for Roman spectators.

Incidentally, we sophisticated members of Western society have our own dramatized violence in the forms of video games and movies that are sometimes even more violent that the Roman games. How far can we be from the real thing?

By the fourth century after Christ, the games had become culturally accepted. Schools for gladiators flourished. Popular combatants could become wealthy and were admired like rock stars today. Hundreds died routinely in gruesome competitions and public executions. It was as much a part of Roman culture as NFL football in America or soccer in most of the rest of the world.

In 404 AD, a hermit monk by the name of Telemachus traveled to Rome just in time to attend the games celebrating a great Roman victory, possibly General Stilicho's defeat of the Visigoths under Alaric. The history of this praiseworthy event is somewhat fuzzy, but the broad facts are as follows:

As Telemachus watched the violence of the games on that January 1st of 404 AD, he was overcome with the cruelty of it all. He was a poor, elderly, ascetic monk who had committed his life to holiness. The brutality of what he watched stirred his spirit as he listened to thousands of cheering fans encouraging men to slaughter one another.

Telemachus made his way to the floor of the arena and personally separated the gladiators as he called to the crowd to stop the bloodshed because it was an insult to God. It is not clear exactly what followed, but it is known that the crowd was angry with his interruption and Telemachus was killed, either by stoning or stabbing and his frail, body lay on the sand bloody and broken.

Telemachus had died, but not in vain. The shock of his death turned the hearts of Romans, including the Emperor Honorarius, who issued an edict banning gladiatorial combats. The games of January 1, 404 AD were the last officially sanctioned games in the Roman Empire. The self-sacrifice of one humble, obscure, almost nameless man was the utterly praiseworthy act that brought an end to six or more centuries of barbaric, public violence.

Think about what is praiseworthy.

"Let us now praise famous men ..."
-Ecclesiasticus 44:1

**For it is commendable if a man bears up
under the pain of unjust suffering
because he is conscious of God.
1 Peter 2:19**

It is good to praise men who are famous for their works of goodness and courage and righteousness. It is equally good to praise obscure men who display the same virtues. One of those men is buried in the words of the prophet Jeremiah's writing. He is seldom if ever mentioned in sermons or painted in murals or sung about in hymns and yet his actions clearly meet the standard of praiseworthiness. His name was Ebed-Melech. He was a servant—possibly a slave—of King Zedekiah, the last king of Judah, and he was a black man in an Israelite culture that came to the rescue of an Israelite man suffering unjustly. That suffering Israelite man was Jeremiah.

Jeremiah was a prophet and in that role he was a constant irritation to the last four kings of Judah. The northern kingdom of Israel had been taken into captivity by the Assyrians nearly a hundred years earlier and then folded into the Assyrian culture to be forever lost to history as the "Ten Lost Tribes." They were not so much lost as they were assimilated so thoroughly as to lose their identity forever. Only the two tribes of Judah and Benjamin were left to make up the southern kingdom of Judah with Jerusalem as the capital.

From 608 BC, through the reigns of Jehoahaz, Jehoiakim and Jehoiachin, to the fall of Jerusalem in 587 BC under the last king, Zedekiah, Jeremiah was a constant irritation to those in civil authority.

In 609 BC, Josiah, the last righteous king of Judah, was killed by an Egyptian archer in the battle of Megiddo. After that, the nation declined spiritually and physically until 605 BC, when Babylon became a single super power in the area under the leadership of Nebuchadnezzar.

Nebuchadnezzar was determined to conquer Judah and its capital, Jerusalem. In fact, God planned that to happen as chastisement for the Jews who had become pagan idolaters. God's consistent advice to the last four kings of Judah through the words of Jeremiah was to surrender to Babylon and accept their captivity. This put Jeremiah in the dangerous position of sounding like a traitor and a collaborator although he was, in fact, speaking the word that God gave him.

During the reign of the last king, Zedekiah, God gave this prophecy to Jeremiah, *"Whoever stays in this city (Jerusalem) will die by the sword, famine or plague, but whoever goes over to the Babylonians will live. He will escape with his life; he will live. This city will certainly be handed over to the army of the king of Babylon, who will capture it"(Jeremiah 38:2-3).*

Zedekiah's lackeys thought this sounded like treason and persuaded Zedekiah to have Jeremiah thrown into a cistern to die. They lowered him into that underground water tank where he sank into the slimy bottom and then they left him in the cold and dark to starve to death. And he would have expired there, cold, wet and forgotten, unless Ebed-Melech, the black foreigner in Zedekiah's court, had done a praiseworthy thing. Actually, Ebed-Melech's actions were praiseworthy on three levels.

First, this foreign servant of the king mustered the courage to confront Zedekiah over his decision to eliminate Jeremiah. In doing this, Ebed-Melech contradicted a cabal of powerful court officials who went over their head to the king at great risk to himself. Men of position and authority normally don't like to be contradicted and Eded-Melech would have known that well, but he was risking his personal safety to rescue another. *"Very rarely will anyone die for a righteous man, though for a good man someone might possibly dare to die"* (Romans 5:7).

When Ebed-Melech received the king's permission to rescue Jeremiah, he went directly to the job of rescuing the prophet. Well, almost directly ...

On the way Ebed-Melech stopped at an old storeroom to gather some rags before he went to the cistern to pull Jeremiah out with stout ropes. That was the second level of his praiseworthy act. He knew that pulling Jeremiah out of the mire with ropes would not be difficult, but it would be painful, so he stopped to find something to ease the discomfort. Jeremiah had been deprived of sun and subject to moisture and bacteria in the cistern and Ebed-Melech was sensitive enough to recognize that his skin would be raw and the rescue would be painful. This courageous servant had a praiseworthy sense of compassion for the suffering Jeremiah.

Finally, Ebed-Melech took some strong rope to extract the prophet from his stinking mud hole at the bottom of the dark cistern. This third element of his praiseworthy action was all about rescue and safety. He needed tough ropes and strong men and he took both.

Ebed-Melech's actions are a subtle lesson in rescuing the perishing. For some, it is natural to throw down a rope of rescue without any compassion. "You got yourself into this mess and here I am to rescue you. Just grab that rope and hold on." Yank. Heave. Ouch.

For others it is normal to avoid anything unpleasant. "Here's a bunch of nice soft rags. Be comforted. Bless your heart. See you later."

Ebed-Melech is a praiseworthy example of one who takes a serious risk and then commits to the hard work of rescue, but with the compassion of the One who saves us. *"I waited patiently for the LORD; he turned to me and heard my cry. He lifted me out of the slimy pit, out of the mud and mire; he set my feet on a rock and gave me a firm place to stand"* (Psalm 40:1-2).

Think about what is praiseworthy.

> "Ridicule is generally made use of to laugh
> men out of virtue and good sense,
> by attacking everything
> praiseworthy in human life."
> -Joseph Addison

**But how is it to your credit if you receive a
beating for doing wrong and endure it? But if
you suffer for doing good and you endure it,
this is commendable before God.
1 Peter 2:20**

Some praiseworthy acts are accomplished in the dark where no one notices. These actions are particularly commendable because they are done with no hope of recognition or praise; they are just the natural behavior of people who are committed to the singular task of pleasing the God who has demonstrated His love for them. These are particularly praiseworthy.

Richard Wurmbrand was born to a Jewish family in 1909 in Bucharest, Romania. His father died when he was 9. When he was 15 (1924) he was sent to study Marxism in Moscow, but he returned secretly to Bucharest a year later disillusioned with Marxism. There he was arrested by the secret police for his political views and briefly imprisoned.

In 1936, he married his wife, Sabina, and in 1938 they both converted to Christianity. In time he was ordained as an Anglican priest and later as a Lutheran pastor, ministering to his native Romanians during WWII.

In 1945, after the Russian domination of Romania at the end of the war, he expanded his ministry to include Russian soldiers. This continued until 1948 when he was arrested on his way to conduct a church service. He was passed through a dozen prison facilities (the communists never lacked for penal institutions to punish Christians, Jews or anyone who disagreed with the state) and finally to the Jilava prison where he spent three years in solitary confinement during which his only human contact was with his communist torturers.

While in solitary, Pastor Wurmbrand lived in squalid conditions, without books or other comforts and often in total darkness. During this time when many would lose their sanity or surrender to self-pity he made it his practice each day to mentally compose a fresh sermon. When the sermon was fully developed in his mind he would deliver it aloud to the darkness and when he had delivered it he would memorize an outline of it. His spiritual and mental discipline was worthy of great praise.

In all, Pastor Wurmbrand spent 14 years in communist prisons because he was a Christ follower. During this time his wife was repeatedly told he was dead and she and her son were harassed and persecuted. In 1950, Sabina was arrested and spent three years at hard labor where she worked with thousands of other women to construct a canal between the Danube River and the Black Sea. These women worked outside in all weather with inadequate clothing and food. The canal project was supported by up to a million slave laborers and has been described by historians as "a cesspool of human suffering and mortality."

During these three years, Sabina spent whatever energy and time she had left to minister to her fellow prisoners with the hope of the Gospel of Christ and the tender encouragements of a woman of great heart and strength of character.

When the Wurmbrands were released in 1964, they eventually traveled to the United States and established a mission that would become known as "Voice of the Martyrs," a ministry that initially served the oppressed in communist countries and grew to help persecuted believers in other places, especially Muslim countries. Together they penned some 20 books, the best known of which are "Tortured for Christ" and "Pastor's Wife." Richard Wurmbrand died February 17, 2001, followed by Sabina's death on August 11, 2001.

Surely in all those years of torture and prison and harassment this couple must have encountered thoughts of revenge and bitterness and hatred. Surely the walls of their minds must have seemed fragile in the face of a battering army of resentful and hostile thoughts, and yet their walls were strong and their gates well built. We cannot know their minds, but their actions suggest that they had uncommon success in thinking about things that were *true, noble, right, pure, lovely, admirable, excellent,* and in the process, modeled for us something that was *praiseworthy.*

> "Praise God, from Whom all blessings flow;
> Praise Him, all creatures here below;
> Praise Him above, ye heavenly host;
> Praise Father, Son, and Holy Ghost."
> -Thomas Ken

Praise the LORD. Praise God in his sanctuary;
praise him in his mighty heavens.
Let everything that has breath praise the LORD.
Praise the LORD.
Psalm 150:1, 6

In the end, everything we find worthy of praise has its roots in God. Telemachus, Eded-Melech, Richard and Sabina Wurmbrand and countless others who have conducted themselves in manners that are truly praiseworthy were all led and sustained and empowered by the God of the universe who is the fountain of all goodness.

As you oversee the gates of your mind to admit thoughts that are praiseworthy, be sure that thoughts of God's majesty, wisdom, mercy, grace and justice are first in line. Once those have been admitted through the gate they will attract countless others.

Think about what is praiseworthy.

"There's the wonder of sunset at evening,
The wonder as sunrise I see;
But the wonder of wonders that thrills my soul
Is the wonder that God loves me."
-George Beverly Shea

**In love he predestined us to be adopted as his
sons through Jesus Christ, in accordance with
his pleasure and will—to the praise of his
glorious grace, which he has freely given us in
the One he loves.
Ephesians 1:5-6**

Eight Stone Gates

Chapter Eleven

Taking Thoughts Captive

"You have absolute control over but
one thing and that is your thoughts.
This is the most significant and
inspiring of all facts known to man!
It reflects man's divine nature."
-Napoleon Hill

**May ... the meditation of my heart be pleasing
in your sight, O LORD, my Rock
and my Redeemer.
Psalm 19:14**

We started this book with a reminder of Nehemiah returning from captivity in Babylon to rebuild the destroyed walls of Jerusalem. The walls had been breached by the army of Nebuchadnezzar in 586 BC, the gates had been destroyed by fire and the whole lot had been subjected to 70 years of neglect and abuse. The Holy City of Jerusalem was left exposed to all the potential harms of hooligans and wild beasts because the walls and gates were ruined.

It is a vivid picture of a human mind that has been neglected. The mental walls are down so that harmful and destructive thoughts just enter at will; thoughts of petty gossip, lingering bitterness, lust, greed, pride and more. Then, even if there is a strong personal commitment to rebuild the walls—to rebuild the spiritual commitments that we understand will be our defense—it is important to mentally erect stout gates which can be shut to exclude wrong and harmful thoughts in the future.

Think about it. If you commanded an ancient city you would want to be sure the walls were well maintained and the gates secure. You would be careful to exclude spies and criminals and agitators and just as keen to welcome honest merchants, loyal soldiers and skilled tradesmen.

Now since you are truly in command of your mind it is important to admit only those thoughts that are beneficial and exclude those that are destructive. You need stout walls and sturdy gates, and those gates are named *true, noble, right, pure, lovely, admirable, excellent and praiseworthy—think about such things.*

"Life does not consist mainly—or even
largely—of facts and happenings. It consists
of the storm of thoughts that is forever
blowing through one's head."
-Mark Twain

**We take captive every thought to make
it obedient to Christ.
2 Corinthians 10:5b**

But here is the difficulty. Our minds are assaulted with thoughts at every instant of waking life. There is never a time when we are not thinking. It is a continuous process from birth to death. If our mental walls and gates are destroyed, thoughts simply enter and leave at will drifting through our minds like a breeze: *"Wish I could afford that new car ... look at that Victoria's Secret advertisement ... if God is love why do orphans starve...need to lose weight... that new guy/gal in the office is cute ... pizza for dinner again ... for God so loved the world ... what time is it ... great game last night ... the Lord is my shepherd ... should paint the bedroom ... hope it's a nice weekend ..."*

And precisely because we are fallen creatures the natural flow is for good thoughts to leave and wrong thoughts to enter. If our mind is left unprotected the net effect will be destructive. Therefore, we are left with only two options: live with an undisciplined and decayed mind, or take control of our thoughts. It is a choice. And we know that God has anticipated the problem and offered the wise counsel to *"take captive every thought to make it obedient to Christ."*

"He that will not command his thoughts will
soon lose the command of his actions."
-Thomas Wilson

**Rejoice in the Lord always.
I will say it again: Rejoice! ...
And the peace of God, which transcends all
understanding, will guard your hearts and
your minds in Christ Jesus.
Philippians 4:4, 7**

One challenge we have in this process is overcoming the prevailing psychological thought that we are victims of our minds; that we cannot really control the thought process and, accordingly, we are subject to the mental whims of our thinking without any defense. That "victim" theory is a bit of academic silliness based on theories of assumptions about conjectures. Even a child knows he can discipline his thoughts; they do it every day in school as they are required to process new information. Just reading this page and digesting the ideas it contains is a form of mental discipline. Indeed, we can control our thoughts, although the process can be strenuous and tiring. Defending the gates always is.

In 480 BC, a Persian army of perhaps a million men under King Xerxes I (the husband of Esther), arrived in Greece to punish and conquer. It may have been the largest army ever assembled until that time; a million or more men in an age when large armies measured in tens of thousands.

Eight Stone Gates

In August of that year, the allied Greek armies decided to block the Persian advance at a place called "The Hot Gates" (Thermopylae), a mountain pass that the historian Herodotus described as being just large enough for a single cart to pass. It was their intention to protect the southern part of Greece by stopping the Persians at this narrow pass that formed a natural entrance through which the Persians would have to advance. If the Spartans could hold the Persians outside of that mountain pass they would protect their land. It was a classic battle to keep the enemy outside by defending a gate. It takes courage to do that, and determination and sacrifice and planning. Defending the gates is never easy.

Because the gate called Thermopylae was a narrow pass, the Spartan King Leonidas took just 300 of his best soldiers and a few others to resist the entire Persian army. He could do that because the walls (the surround terrain) were strong and impregnable and the gate (Thermopylae) was narrow. It was a few hundred determined Spartans against hundreds of thousands of Persians.

The battle of Thermopylae lasted seven days, three of them long days of intense, hand to hand combat. Leonidas and his men courageously defended the gate until a traitor named Ephialtes showed the Persians another route around the Greeks, and in the end all of the Spartans were slaughtered.

Thermopylae is a vivid picture of the battles sometimes necessary to defend the gates. It is also a picture of the scheming traitors who will undermine our efforts. Taking thoughts captive to keep them from entering the gates can be hard work, but Paul also made it clear that we live in a spiritual battle and should therefore suit up in spiritual armor and that we can win. See the sixth chapter of Ephesians.

No one said this was easy. They did say it was right and good and pleasing to God. What more do we need? *We take captive every thought to make it obedient to Christ.*

> "Man is obviously made to think. It is his
> whole dignity and his whole merit; and
> his whole duty is to think as he ought."
> -Pascal

"What do you think?"
Matthew 18:12

Good question. "What do you think?" Jesus asked that question of his disciples several times during His ministry. He could just as easily have asked:
"What is going on in your head?"
"What are your basic assumptions?"
"What is distracting you?"
"What traditions and folklore are you applying to this situation?"
"Are you making any effort to process this and make something coherent out of it or are you just playing games?"

"What do you think?"

Paul was speaking bedrock truth when he reminded us that we live immersed in a spiritual battle, which actually begins in the mind: *"our struggle is not against flesh and blood, but against the rulers, against the authorities, against the powers of this dark world and against the spiritual forces of evil in the heavenly realms"* (Ephesians 6:12).

"What do you think?" Christians are routinely exposed to corrosive thinking as they attempt to live out a life that is consistent with their convictions. There are a multitude of possibilities. Consider:

- Ignorance.   We are beset by a barrage of accumulated ignorance on a number of subjects. Information swirls through the internet and text messages and email, TV and talk radio, gossip and water-cooler conversation, gathering distortions and error as it travels like a snowball. We are confronted with conspiracy theories, bogus medical cures, questionable investment advice and gross distortions of history on a daily basis. Much of this misinformation can be wrong, harmful or both. It is our responsibility to *take captive every thought to make it obedient to Christ.* Think about what is true.

- Counterfeit wisdom.   We are exposed to popular wisdom (which is frequently not wisdom at all) on the desirability of divorce, the personal need for self-esteem, the supposed error of child discipline and our personal hierarchy of "needs," none of which are based on biblical knowledge or wisdom. These thoughts clamor at the gates, supported by encouraging throngs, demanding entry. *We take captive every thought to make it obedient to Christ.* Think about what is right.

- Evil.   There are the simply evil thoughts that demand entry: thoughts of lust, greed, envy, bitterness, unforgiveness, pride, impatience, self-indulgence, fear, worry and anxiety, hatred, cruelty, spite, revenge, eroticism and more. Every mind has a different and distinct alliance of enemies which gather outside the walls and seek entry. *We take captive every thought to make it obedient to Christ.* Think about what is pure.

- Misunderstandings.   Finally, there are serious misunderstandings that lurk at the gates: thoughts that we can somehow work our way into God's eternal presence; thoughts that we are not really so bad after all; thoughts about how clever we are and independent and resourceful and smart and good; thoughts that life and behavior are (or should be) fundamentally good; thoughts that Jesus was a good teacher, but no more. All of these thoughts deny the simple fact that we live in a fallen and corrupt world, that we are born in sin and desperately need a Savior and that we have nothing that is not a gift from God. *We take captive every thought to make it obedient to Christ.* Think about what is noble.

What do you think? Without mental and spiritual discipline our thoughts degenerate from the Godly to the base, from the virtuous to the vulgar. It is the natural order of things, and for that very reason it is important to take on the active and deliberate challenge to *take captive every thought to make it obedient to Christ.*

> "God will not discipline us, we must discipline
> ourselves. God will not bring every
> thought and imagination into captivity;
> we must do it."
> -Oswald Chambers

**Furthermore, since they did not think it
worthwhile to retain the knowledge of God,
he gave them over to a depraved mind to
do what ought not to be done.
Romans 1:28**

Thinking is easy. Right thinking is the hardest work, and yet everything in life stems from what we think and what we believe.

It is no small task to erect sturdy walls of personal commitment around our mind and to maintain secure gates for continuous filtering to eliminate harmful and invalid thoughts, and yet that is exactly what God had in mind when he gave those words to Paul ...

**Finally, brothers, whatever is true, whatever
is noble, whatever is right, whatever is pure,
whatever is lovely, whatever is admirable—
if anything is excellent or praiseworthy—
think about such things.
Philippians 4:8,**

and

**We take captive every thought to make it
obedient to Christ.
2 Corinthians 10:5b**

Think of your mind as being surrounded by a wall of God's protection. He has provided that wall as a means for all who count Jesus Christ alone as their Savior and Lord to exclude sinful thoughts while leaving gateways for right thoughts to enter. Remember that the city is always under attack by powerful and destructive forces that constantly seek entrance, but the goal is to keep a strong and diligent guard to filter our thoughts through these eight stone gates:

- The Truth Gate is where we allow only information that is carefully validated and certified to be true. The Truth Gate is for admitting <u>thoughts of what is</u>.
- The Noble Gate is where thoughts of courage, generosity and honor are admitted. The Noble Gate is for admitting <u>thoughts of the good that could be</u>.
- The Right Gate is for thoughts that are proper and appropriate for a son of the King. The Right Gate is designed for <u>thoughts of what should be</u>.
- The Pure Gate is designed for thoughts that are free of impurities and contaminants. The Pure Gate is for <u>thoughts of what ought to be</u>.
- The Lovely Gate is for inspiring thoughts of beauty and delight, both physical and moral. The Lovely Gate is for <u>thoughts of God and whatever draws us toward Him</u>.

- The Admirable Gate is for thoughts of things that are inspiring and deserving of high praise and approval. The Admirable Gate is for <u>thoughts of those things of which we are capable</u>.
- The Excellent Gate is for thoughts of things that possess outstanding qualities; things that are remarkably good. The Excellent Gate is for <u>thoughts of those things to which we should aspire</u>.
- The Praiseworthy Gate is for thoughts of things that are highly commendable; things that are worthy of applause and tribute. The Praiseworthy Gate is for <u>thoughts of things that are inspiring and motivating</u>.

Ordering, instructing and disciplining our thoughts is a challenge. It is a challenge that lasts a lifetime. It is a challenge that pleases God and protects our mind and heart.

It is a challenge worth taking, and if you would like to begin, the Appendix that follows is designed for that. Nehemiah spent 52 days repairing the walls and gates of Jerusalem after they had been destroyed and then neglected for 70 years. You can repair your walls and gates in 52 days if you are willing to step out in faith and trust God for the help He has always promised. The appendix is intended for that very project.

Whether you accept that 52 day challenge or not, remember that wars are not won behind gates and walls. Those defenses are crucial to protect vital interests, but wars are eventually won by vigorous offensive campaigns which take the fight onto enemy territory. Our warfare can begin with rebuilt walls and restored gates, but those are intended to create the secure base from which we can launch out into dynamic action in the everyday battles of life.

Your mind is the repository of spiritual resources for good or evil. Protect it well. Restore the walls. Rebuild the gates and put them to good use. And then launch out into aggressive offense against the enemies that attack you daily.

"Associate reverently, as much as you can,
with your loftiest thoughts."
-Henry David Thoreau

**Whatever is true, noble, right, pure, lovely,
admirable, excellent or praiseworthy—
think about such things.
Philippians 4:8** (paraphrase)

Appendix

Fifty Two Days (or weeks) of Building Walls and Hanging Gates

The prophet Nehemiah is our inspiration for this challenge. 450 years before Christ, Nehemiah returned to his beloved city of Jerusalem to find that the walls and gates were destroyed. The city was wide open to any predator that came along and it had lapsed into a neglected state of ruin, populated by a few dispirited people contending with enemy tribes, rats, snakes, wild dogs and other predators. Jerusalem was a mess because it had no means of defense.

Our mind is like that. Without walls and gates to defend it, the mind becomes infested with lies, deceptions and a remarkable assortment of corrupt thinking.

Nehemiah rallied the people of Jerusalem to rebuild the walls and gates even in the face of serious opposition by hostile neighbors. At one point the builders had to work with a weapon in one hand and a tool in the other, but they persevered and the work was completed in 52 days. It was an amazing feat inspired by Nehemiah's encouragement: *"Don't be afraid of them. Remember the Lord, who is great and awesome, and fight for your brothers, your sons and your daughters, your wives and your homes." (Nehemiah 4:14 NIV)*

When they were done, the city had the means by which to defend itself so that the predators and marauders within the walls could be expelled and those outside could be kept there. The walls and gates created the basic means to achieve a safe city.

Our minds are like that. Once we have built the walls of a personal relationship with God through His Savior Son Jesus Christ, and hung the gates of right thinking described in Philippians 4:8, we have the means to exclude the harmful and admit the good and wise. And while this process may require strenuous effort we need not be afraid because we can *"Remember the Lord, who is great and awesome, and fight for our brothers, our sons and our daughters, our wives and our homes." (Nehemiah 4:14 NIV)*

So, just as Nehemiah built the walls and gates in 52 days, this challenge is designed for 52 days (or weeks if you prefer) of dedicated personal work of rebuilding the walls and hanging the gates that are necessary for mental and spiritual well being. If you are a believer in Jesus Christ the walls are there. They may need repair and reinforcement and that will be part of the challenge. But for all of us there is the constant struggle to keep the gates in good repair so that our thoughts can be filtered through those eight biblical apertures described by Paul.

"To map out a course of action and follow it
to an end requires courage."
-Ralph Waldo Emerson

**Finally, brothers, whatever is true, whatever
is noble, whatever is right, whatever is pure,
whatever is lovely, whatever is admirable—
if anything is excellent or praiseworthy—
think about such things.
Philippians 4:8**

**You need to persevere so that when
you have done the will of God, you
will receive what he has promised.
Hebrews 10:36**

**Let us run with perseverance the
race marked out for us.
Hebrews 12:1b**

The 52 day (or week) challenge that follows is arranged in
the same order as the book in general. For each day, you will
find a thought and a verse for consideration and meditation.
These are intended for careful consideration over time, whether
that is an entire day or the whole week, they are designed to
focus your thinking rather than just fill a moment of morning
reading. It is helpful to make a copy, cut out that day's (week's)
challenge and post it conspicuously until it is time for the next;
and so forth.

In each case, the thought and verse are related to a portion of
the book so that the challenge follows the general outline of the
text. In many cases, the thought and the verse are repeated from
the appropriate section of the book but they are included here as
an encouragement to think more deeply about them and, if you
are courageous enough, to commit the Bible verse to memory.
Remember that at all times you will need a tool in one hand
(prayer, wise counsel, fellowship and personal commitment)
and a weapon in the other (thought and verse of the day or
week).

So, are you willing? There are 52 units of construction
ahead, but if you persist—if you persevere—in the end you will
have walls and gates that are sufficiently robust to protect your
thinking from the general corruption of the world. It is time to
begin because *"The end of (this) matter is better than its beginning"*
(Ecclesiastes 7:8).

Building the Walls (From Chapter One)

Five days are devoted to considering the importance of this
challenge to build mental walls and gates designed to exclude

damaging and wrong thoughts. Censorship has been given a bad name by those who believe that all thoughts are valid, but no wise person entertains all thoughts, and they are not all equally valid. There are noble thoughts and ignoble thoughts and only strong gates and walls can separate the two.

Day 1 "Temptation usually comes in through a door that has deliberately been left open." -Arnold Glasow	You see the trouble we are in: Jerusalem lies in ruins, and its gates have been burned with fire. Come, let us rebuild the wall of Jerusalem, and we will no longer be in disgrace (Nehemiah 2:17).
Day 2 "Men of sense often learn from their enemies. It is from their foes, not their friends, that cities learn the lesson of building high walls and ships of war." -Aristophanes	You will call your walls Salvation and your gates Praise. Isaiah 60:18
Day 3 "Before I built a wall I'd ask to know what I was walling in or walling out." -Robert Frost	Your people will rebuild the ancient ruins and will raise up the age-old foundations; you will be called Repairer of Broken Walls. Isaiah 58:12

Day 4 "Happiness is like those palaces in fairy tales whose gates are guarded by dragons." -Alexandre Dumas	Open for me the gates of righteousness; I will enter and give thanks to the LORD. Psalm 118:19
Day 5 "Good thoughts are blessed guests, and should be heartily welcomed, well fed and much sought after. Like rose leaves they give out a sweet smell if laid up in the jar of memory." -Charles Spurgeon	I went past the field of the sluggard ... the ground was covered with weeds, and the stone wall was in ruins. Proverbs 24:30-31

The Problem with Thinking (From Chapter Two)

Five days are devoted to the simple issue of our constant and unrelenting stream of thought. There is no such thing as an empty mind; it is always full and the challenge is to fill it with good and noble thoughts because what you think is the foundation for what you do.

Day 6 "Every man has a train of thought on which he travels when he is alone. The dignity and nobility of his life, as well as his happiness, depend upon the direction in which that train is going, the baggage it carries, and the scenery through which it travels." -Joseph Fort Newton	Brothers, stop thinking like children. In regard to evil be infants, but in your thinking be adults. 1 Corinthians 14:20
Day 7 "Thoughts lead on to purposes; purposes go forth in action; actions form habits; habits decide character; and character fixes our destiny." -Tryon Edwards	Finally, brothers, whatever is true, whatever is noble, whatever is right, whatever is pure, whatever is lovely, whatever is admirable—if anything is excellent or praiseworthy—think about such things. Philippians 4:8

Day 8 "Thoughts may be bandits. Thoughts may be raiders. Thoughts may be invaders. Thoughts may be disturbers of the international peace." -Woodrow Wilson	When I was a child, I talked like a child; I thought like a child, I reasoned like a child. When I became a man, I put childish ways behind me. 1 Corinthians 13:11
Day 9 "Thought precedes action as lightning does thunder." -Heinrich Heine	For as he thinks in his heart, so is he. Proverbs 23:7 (NKJV)
Day 10 "I can easily conceive of a man without hands, feet or head, for it is only experience that teaches us that the head is more necessary than the feet. But, I cannot conceive of a man without thoughts; he would be a stone or a brute." -Blaise Pascal	So I tell you this, and insist on it in the Lord, that you must no longer live as the Gentiles do, in the futility of their thinking. Ephesians 4:17

Eight Stone Gates

The Gate of True Thoughts (From Chapter Three)

Five days are devoted to building a mind gate designed to exclude all thoughts that are not true. The goal is to think about what is verifiable, demonstrable or provable; thoughts that are not legend and story, rumor and gossip, hearsay and anecdote. Thoughts that conform to the reality of things. The Truth Gate is where we allow only information that is carefully validated and certified to be true. The Truth Gate is for admitting thoughts of what is.

Day 11 "The question is not whether a doctrine is beautiful but whether it is true. When we wish to go to a place, we do not ask whether the road leads through a pretty country, but whether it is the right road." -A.W. and J.C. Hare	Surely you desire truth in the inner parts. Psalm 51:6
Day 12 "To treat your facts with imagination is one thing; to imagine your facts is another." -John Burroughs	Love does not delight in evil but rejoices with the truth. 1 Corinthians 13:6

Day 13 The truth, the whole truth and nothing but the truth." -Legal phrase from at least 1300AD	Buy the truth and do not sell it. Proverbs 23:23
Day 14 "Truth is as impossible to soil by any outward touch as the sunbeam." -John Milton	For the law was given through Moses; grace and truth came through Jesus Christ. John 1:17
Day 15 "Truth is truth 'til the end of reckoning." -Shakespeare	You shall know the truth and the truth shall set you free. John 8:32

The Gate of Noble Thoughts (From Chapter Four)

Five days are dedicated to building a gate for noble thoughts. Your Bible translation may use the word "honest" or "honorable." Some translations use the English word "grave" in the sense of serious and important. The notion here is of a quality that is noble and momentous and worthy of reverence before God. It is not some flimsy code of "nobility" that emerges from human tradition, but an honor that can stand the test of eternity. It is noble in the very best sense; noble as Christ was noble in all that He did. It is noble as in being majestic and awe-inspiring in a way that invites and attracts. Think about what is noble.

Day 16 "A noble man compares and estimates himself by an idea which is higher than himself; and a mean man, by one lower than himself." -Henry Ward Beecher	But the noble man makes noble plans, and by noble deeds he stands. Isaiah 32:8
Day 17 "The purpose of life is not to be happy. It is to be useful, to be honorable, to be compassionate, to have it make some difference that you have lived and lived well." -Ralph Waldo Emerson	But the seed on good soil stands for those with a noble and good heart, who hear the word, retain it, and by persevering produce a crop. Luke 8:15

Day 18 "There is no more noble occupation in the world than to assist another human being—to help someone succeed." -Alan Loy McGinnis	Be devoted to one another in brotherly love. Honor one another above yourselves. Romans 12:10
Day 19 "I long to accomplish a great and noble task, but it is my chief duty to accomplish humble tasks as though they were great and noble" -Helen Keller	Live such good lives among the pagans that, though they accuse you of doing wrong, they may see your good deeds and glorify God on the day he visits us. 1 Peter 2:12
Day 20 "Every noble crown is, and on earth will forever be, a crown of thorns." -Thomas Carlyle	Blessed is the man who perseveres under trial, because when he has stood the test, he will receive the crown of life that God has promised to those who love him. James 1:12

Eight Stone Gates

The Gate of Right Thoughts (From Chapter Five)

Five days are given to build the gate of right thoughts. "Right," along with "fair" and "just" and "righteous" in this context, are important attributes for the thoughts we want to admit into our minds. This gate is where we screen out thoughts that are biased or prejudiced or unfair. The Right Gate is for thoughts that are proper and appropriate for a son of the King. What follows are five thoughts and five verses to help define a gate for right thoughts.

Day 21 "For right is right, since God is God, and right the day must win. To doubt would be disloyalty, to falter would be sin." -F.W Faber	This is the gate of the LORD through which the righteous may enter. Psalm 118:19-20
Day 22 "Rightness expresses in actions what straightness does in lines; and there can no more be two kinds of right action than there can be two kinds of straight lines." -Herbert Spencer	There is a way that seems right to a man, but in the end it leads to death. Proverbs 14:12

Day 23 "The line between good and evil runs directly through the heart of every man and woman." -Aleksandr Solzhenitsyn	Create in me a clean heart, O God; and renew a right spirit within me. Psalm 51:10
Day 24 Let us have faith that right makes might and in that faith let us to the end dare to do our duty as we understand it." -Abraham Lincoln	The way of the LORD is a refuge for the righteous. Proverbs 10:29
Day 25 "There is always a right and a wrong way and the wrong way always seems the more reasonable." -George Moore	The path of the righteous is like the first gleam of dawn, shining ever brighter till the full light of day. Proverbs 4:18

Eight Stone Gates

The Gate of Pure Thoughts (From Chapter Six)

Five days will be used to construct a gate for pure thoughts. The Pure Gate is designed for thoughts that are free of impurities and contaminants. Purity is a highly desired quality in food, air, medicine, science and manufacturing. It should be the same with our thoughts.

Only serious heart work can purify our thoughts, and out of that pure heart will come pure words and deeds. Surely, this is not a strange concept because you can remember those times in the past when you drove home from church, yelled at the children, criticized a neighbor, yelled at an inconsiderate driver, or even roasted the preacher with your criticism. Purity is an internal matter, which requires diligence and detail only available through the help of the Holy Spirit. Think about what is pure.

Day 26 "A pure mind in a chaste body is the mother of wisdom." -Jeremy Taylor	Everyone who has this hope in him purifies himself, just as He is pure. 1 John 3:3
Day 27 "God would not rub so hard if it were not to fetch out the dirt that is ingrained in our natures. God loves purity so well He had rather see a hole than a spot in His child's garments." -William Gurnall	Create in me a pure heart, O God. Psalm 51:10

Day 28 "Simplicity reaches out after God; purity discovers and enjoys Him." -Thomas A Kempis	Everyone who has this hope in Him purifies himself, just as he is pure. 1 John 3:3
Day 29 "There is a difference between innocence and purity. Innocence is the characteristic of a child; purity is the characteristic of a man or woman who knows what the tendencies and temptations to go wrong are and who has overcome them." -Oswald Chambers	Keep yourself pure. 1 Timothy 5:22b
Day 30 "Like the stained cloth that whitens in the sun, grow pure by being shone upon." -Thomas Moore	Since we have these promises, dear friends, let us purify ourselves from everything that contaminates body and spirit, perfecting holiness out of reverence for God. 2 Corinthians 7:1

Eight Stone Gates

The Gate of Lovely Thoughts (From Chapter Seven)

These five days will help to erect a gate that attracts lovely thinking. "Lovely" in the original Greek has the meaning of those things that move us toward affection. They are thoughts that inspire and encourage and leave us with a sense of appreciation for their intrinsic excellence. The Lovely Gate is for inspiring thoughts of beauty and delight, both physical and moral. The Lovely Gate is for thoughts of God and His creation. Think about what is lovely.

Day 31 "You are altogether lovely, altogether worthy, Altogether wonderful to me, my Lord." -Timothy David Hughes	Who among the gods is like you, O LORD? Who is like you—majestic in holiness, awesome in glory, working wonders? Exodus 15:11
Day 32 "Why should we think upon things that are lovely? Because thinking determines life." -William James	Have this mind in you, which was also in Christ Jesus. Philippians 2:5

Day 33 "Every man feels instinctively that all the beautiful sentiments in the world weigh less than a single lovely action." -James Russell Lowell	Why are you bothering this woman? (Who has anointed me with perfume.) She has done a beautiful thing to me. Matthew 26:10
Day 34 "Silently, one by one, in the infinite meadows of heaven, blossomed the lovely stars, the forget-me-nots of the angel." -Henry Wadsworth Longfellow	On the glorious splendor of your majesty, and on your wondrous works, I will meditate. Psalm 145:5
Day 35 "A Christmas candle is a lovely thing; it makes no noise at all, but softly gives itself away." -Eva Logue	Carry each other's burdens, and in this way you will fulfill the law of Christ. Galatians 6:2

Eight Stone Gates

The Gate of Admirable Thoughts (From Chapter Eight)

Five days are needed to work on the gate that will admit admirable thoughts. Bible translators have used several English words or combinations to grasp the concept of the Greek word Paul uses here, including "good report," "commendable," "good repute," "gracious" and "admirable."

Admirable. The Admirable Gate is for thoughts of things that are inspiring and deserving of high praise and approval. Think about things that are admirable; commendable; worth talking about, and, incidentally, worth thinking about. Whatever is admirable—think about such things.

Day 36 "Men value things in three ways: as useful ... as pleasant or sources of pleasure ... and as intrinsically admirable or honorable." -Mortimer Adler	Whatever is admirable ... think about such things. Philippians 4:8
Day 37 "This is the mark of a really admirable man: steadfastness in the face of trouble." -Ludwig van Beethoven	Let us throw off everything that hinders and the sin that so easily entangles, and let us run with perseverance the race marked out for us. Hebrews 12:1b

Day 38 "Committing a great truth to memory is admirable; committing it to life is wisdom." -William A. Ward	I have hidden your word in my heart that I might not sin against you. Psalm 119:11
Day 39 "We are willing to be pleased but we are not willing to admire." -Samuel Johnson	I will sacrifice a freewill offering to you; I will praise your name, O LORD, for it is good. Psalm 54:6
Day 40 "When I was young I admired clever people. Now that I am old I admire kind people." -Abraham Heschel	Make sure that nobody pays back wrong for wrong, but always try to be kind to each other and to everyone else. 1 Thessalonians 5:15

Eight Stone Gates

The Gate of Excellent Thoughts (From Chapter Nine)

Five days are needed to hang the gate designed to admit excellent thoughts. The Excellent Gate is for thoughts of things that possess outstanding qualities; things that are remarkably good. The Excellent Gate is for thoughts of those things to which we should aspire. It is the kind of excellence that leads people to humility, modesty, purity and other moral virtue, but it conveys a robust and vigorous form of such virtue. This is no wimpy, passive "niceness"; it is a dynamic virtue applied to very real circumstances of life.

Day 41 "The secret of living a life of excellence is merely a matter of thinking thoughts of excellence. Really, it's a matter of programming our minds with the kind of information that will set us free." -Charles R. Swindoll	If anything is excellent ... think about such things. Philippians 4:8 (paraphrase)
Day 42 "I assure you that I would rather excel others in the knowledge of what is excellent, than in the extent of my power and dominion." -Plutarch	Now for this very reason also, applying all diligence, in your faith supply moral excellence, and in your moral excellence, knowledge. 2 Peter 1:5 (NASB)

Day 43 "Mediocrity is never God's will for us. He calls us to excellence and challenges us to be more than we thought." -Max Browning	Think about what is excellent. Philippians 4:8 (paraphrase)
Day 44 "An excellent plumber is infinitely more admirable than an incompetent philosopher. The society which scorns excellence in plumbing because plumbing is a humble activity, and tolerates shoddiness in philosophy because it is an exalted activity, will have neither good plumbing nor good philosophy. Neither its pipes nor its theories will hold water." -John W. Gardner	I want you to stress these things, so that those who have trusted in God may be careful to devote themselves to doing what is good. These things are excellent and profitable for everyone. Titus 3:5
Day 45 "Excellent things are rare." -Plato	And now I will show you the most excellent way. 1 Corinthians 12:31

The Gate of Praiseworthy Thoughts (From Chapter Ten)

So, we come to the eighth and last category of thought that Paul advises in this single verse we are tracing from Philippians 4:8. Using our metaphor of gates mounted in a stone wall, this is the last doorway to be erected and fortified. This is the gate that admits only those thoughts of things that are praiseworthy, commendable, or worthy of compliment. The Praiseworthy Gate is for thoughts of things that are inspiring and motivating.

Day 46 "We participate, in a sense, in noble deeds when we praise them sincerely." -LaRouchefoucauld	We will not hide them from their children; we will tell the next generation the praiseworthy deeds of the LORD. Psalm 78:4
Day 47 "Let us now praise famous men ..." -Ecclesiasticus 44:1	For it is commendable if a man bears up under the pain of unjust suffering because he is conscious of God. 1 Peter 2:19

Day 48 "While it is well enough to leave footprints on the sands of time, it is even more important to make sure they point in a commendable direction." -James Branch Cabell	These (trials) have come so that your faith may be proved genuine and may result in praise, glory and honor when Jesus Christ is revealed. 1 Peter 1:7
Day 49 "Ridicule is generally made use of to laugh men out of virtue and good sense, by attacking everything praiseworthy in human life." -Joseph Addison	But how is it to your credit if you receive a beating for doing wrong and endure it? But if you suffer for doing good and you endure it, this is commendable before God. 1 Peter 2:20
Day 50 "Praise God, from Whom all blessings flow; Praise Him, all creatures here below; Praise Him above, ye heavenly host; Praise Father, Son, and Holy Ghost." -Thomas Ken	Praise the LORD. Praise God in his sanctuary; praise him in his mighty heavens. Let everything that has breath praise the LORD. Praise the LORD. Psalm 150:1, 6

Eight Stone Gates

Taking Thoughts Captive (From Chapter Eleven)

We started this book with a reminder of Nehemiah returning from captivity in Babylon to rebuild the destroyed walls of Jerusalem, a job that was completed in 52 days. The walls had been breached by the army of Nebuchadnezzar in 586 BC, the gates had been destroyed by fire and the whole lot had been subjected to 70 years of neglect and abuse. The holy city of Jerusalem was left exposed to all the potential harms of hooligans and wild beasts because the walls and gates were ruined.

It is a vivid picture of a human mind that has been neglected. The mental walls are down so that harmful and destructive thoughts just enter at will; thoughts of petty gossip, lingering bitterness, lust, greed, pride and more. Then, even if there is a strong personal commitment to rebuild the walls—to rebuild the spiritual commitments that we understand will be our defense—it is important to mentally erect stout gates which can be shut to exclude wrong and harmful thoughts in the future. In the end, it is the deliberate process of taking control of our thoughts.

Day 51 "God will not discipline us, we must discipline ourselves. God will not bring every thought and imagination into captivity; we must do it." -Oswald Chambers	We take captive every thought to make it obedient to Christ. 2 Corinthians 10:5b

Day 52 "You have absolute control over but one thing and that is your thoughts. This is the most significant and inspiring of all facts known to man! It reflects man's divine nature." -Napoleon Hill	May ... the meditation of my heart be pleasing in your sight, O LORD, my Rock and my Redeemer. Psalm 19:14

So, the 52 days (or weeks) are completed. It is not a simple task to rebuild the walls and gates of our minds, but it is a process pleasing to God and valuable to us. Now that the building is complete, it is important to maintain those walls and gates with regular and diligent maintenance.

"This is not the end. It is not even the beginning of the end. But it is, perhaps, the end of the beginning."
-Winston Churchill

The fear of the LORD is the beginning of wisdom.
Proverbs 9:10

Eight Stone Gates

About the Author

Dan Manningham has been married to his wife, Fran, for 51 years. They have 7 children and 28 grandchildren. They are both NANC Certified Biblical Counselors with an active counseling ministry within their church. He is a preaching elder in their local church and occasional speaker at other churches and conferences.

They have served as short term missionaries and/or visited mission fields in Mali (West Africa), Kenya, Tanzania, Papua, Papua New Guinea, Costa Rica and Brazil, and countries in Central Asia.

Dan has served on the Board of Directors at Mission Aviation Fellowship, Mission Safety International, PACTEC, Mansfield Christian School and Richland Pregnancy Services. He is retired after 33 years at United Airlines where his last position was 747 Captain.

Dan has published several hundred articles and three books on aviation safety issues. He is the author of *Six Stone Jars: God's Remedy for Fear, Worry and Anxiety*. He can be contacted by email at stonejars@yahoo.com, or visit his "blog": http://stonebooks.blogspot.com

Eight Stone Gates